"Artfully woven into the fabric of who we are, each of us possesses an urgency to be included, an ache to be known, and a longing to be welcomed. In this book, Rosaria describes how the good news of the gospel not only meets our deepest needs but transforms us into cohosts who invite others to meet Jesus. Rosaria Butterfield's enthusiasm for the unparalleled expression of hospitality—the Son of God on the cross drawing all men to himself—is what energizes her to practice radically ordinary hospitality and invite us all to do the same. This book will stir your imagination to generate creative ways to incorporate radically ordinary hospitality into your own life as well."

Gloria Furman, author, *Missional Motherhood* and *Treasuring Christ When Your Hands Are Full*

"God strongly advances his cause by raising up prophetic voices of fresh insight, bold words, and powerful impact. Rosaria Butterfield is just such a voice for God in our time. *The Gospel Comes with a House Key* is Rosaria's heart reaching out to our hearts, calling us to love our neighbors with sacrificial hospitality. This book is going to shake us all up in the most wonderfully destabilizing way."

Ray Ortlund, Lead Pastor, Immanuel Church, Nashville, Tennessee

"This book isn't for those who want to live the comfortable Christian life. Rosaria proves there is no such thing. She has a unique way of blending personal story and theological teaching that challenges the reader to engage in areas of both agreement and disagreement. I was sharpened well in both cases."

Aimee Byrd, author, *Why Can't We Be Friends?* and *No Little Women*

"It's easier than ever to live in communities with no real sense of community. Neighbors don't know neighbors, and our lives are lived online rather than on the front porch. Rosaria Butterfield demonstrates how living a life of radically ordinary hospitality can allow strangers to become neighbors, and, by God's power, those neighbors can become part of God's family. I couldn't put this book down—it's compelling, challenging, and convicting."

Melissa Kruger, author, *The Envy of Eve* and *Walking with God in the Season of Motherhood*

"One cannot spend any time at all with Rosaria Butterfield without a renewed sense of how good the good news really is. This book is a needed call to the church to model the hospitality of our Lord. As our culture faces a crisis of loneliness, this is the book we need. The book will inspire you and leave you with a notebook filled with ideas for how to practically engage your neighbors with the welcome of the gospel."

Russell Moore, President, The Ethics & Religious Liberties Commission

"The biblical call to show hospitality is one of the most overlooked or misunderstood commands in Scripture. We either ignore it or mistake it for what our culture calls 'entertaining.' Rosaria Butterfield gives us a vision of hospitality that pulses with the beating heart of the gospel itself. We know a God who sought us out, took us in, made us family, and seated us at his table. It's a vision that is bracing and attractive. It daunts us, but it shouldn't. I wonder how different our homes, churches, and culture would look if we took it to heart."

Sam Allberry, author, *Why Bother with Church?* and *Is God Anti-Gay?*

"One of the hallmarks of the people of God is supposed to be hospitality. But in an age of commuter churches, towns disemboweled by shopping malls, and lives that are overscheduled and full of ceaseless activity, hospitality is something which, like true friendship, is at a premium. In this book, Rosaria Butterfield makes a bold case for putting hospitality back into the essential rhythm of the church's daily life. She sets the bar very high—and there is plenty of room here for disagreement on some of the proposals and details—but the basic case, that church is to be a community marked by hospitality, is powerfully presented and persuasively argued."

Carl R. Trueman, William E. Simon Visiting Fellow in Religion and Public Life, Princeton University

The Gospel Comes with a House Key

The Gospel Comes with a House Key

Practicing Radically Ordinary Hospitality in Our Post-Christian World

Rosaria Champagne Butterfield

:: CROSSWAY®

WHEATON, ILLINOIS

The Gospel Comes with a House Key: Practicing Radically Ordinary Hospitality in Our Post-Christian World

Copyright © 2018 by Rosaria Champagne Butterfield

Published by Crossway
        1300 Crescent Street
        Wheaton, Illinois 60187

Published in association with the literary agency of Wolgemuth & Associates, Inc.

Portions of chapter 5, "The Gospel Comes with a House Key: The Seal of Hospitality," are taken from Rosaria Champagne Butterfield, *Openness Unhindered: Further Thoughts of an Unlikely Convert on Sexual Identity and Union with Christ* (Pittsburgh, PA: Crown & Covenant, 2015), 147–64. Used by permission.

Cover design: Micah Lanier

First printing 2018

Printed in the United States of America

Unless otherwise indicated, Scripture quotations are from the ESV® Bible (The Holy Bible, English Standard Version®), copyright © 2001 by Crossway, a publishing ministry of Good News Publishers. Used by permission. All rights reserved.

Scripture quotations marked KJV are from the *King James Version* of the Bible.

Scripture references marked NLT are from *The Holy Bible, New Living Translation*, copyright © 1996, 2004. Used by permission of Tyndale House Publishers, Inc., Wheaton, IL, 60189. All rights reserved.

All emphases in Scripture quotations have been added by the author.

Hardcover ISBN: 978-1-4335-5786-6
ePub ISBN: 978-1-4335-5789-7
PDF ISBN: 978-1-4335-5787-3
Mobipocket ISBN: 978-1-4335-5788-0

Library of Congress Cataloging-in-Publication Data

Names: Butterfield, Rosaria Champagne, 1962- author.
Title: The Gospel comes with a house key : practicing radically ordinary hospitality in our post-Christian world / Rosaria Champagne Butterfield.
Description: Wheaton : Crossway, 2018. | Includes bibliographical references and index.
Identifiers: LCCN 2017031557 (print) | LCCN 2018000815 (ebook) | ISBN 9781433557873 (pdf) | ISBN 9781433557880 (mobi) | ISBN 9781433557897 (epub) | ISBN 9781433557866 (hc)
Subjects: LCSH: Hospitality—Religious aspects—Christianity. | Strangers—Religious aspects—Christianity.
Classification: LCC BV4647.H67 (ebook) | LCC BV4647.H67 B88 2018 (print) | DDC 241/.671—dc23
LC record available at https://lccn.loc.gov/2017031557

For
Kent Butterfield,
faithful husband, leader of our household, father
of our children, my courageous pastor, and
humble disciple of the Lord Jesus Christ.
Not one page of this book could have been
written or lived without you.
This book is for you, with all of my love.

Contents

Preface

Radically ordinary hospitality—those who live it see strangers as neighbors and neighbors as family of God. They recoil at reducing a person to a category or a label. They see God's image reflected in the eyes of every human being on earth. They know they are like meth addicts and sex-trade workers. They take their own sin seriously—including the sin of selfishness and pride. They take God's holiness and goodness seriously. They use the Bible as a lifeline, with no exceptions.

Those who live out radically ordinary hospitality see their homes not as theirs at all but as God's gift to use for the furtherance of his kingdom. They open doors; they seek out the underprivileged. They know that the gospel comes with a house key. They take biblical theology seriously, as well as Christian creeds and confessions and traditions.

Offering radically ordinary hospitality is an everyday thing at our house. It starts early, with minestrone soup simmering on one burner and a pot of steamed rice warming on another. It ends late, with Kent making beds on the couches and blowing up air mattresses for a traveling, stranded family. A truly hospitable heart anticipates everyday, Christ-centered table fellowship and guests who are genuinely in need. Such a heart seeks opportunities to serve. Radically ordinary hospitality doesn't keep fussy lists or make a big deal about invitations. Invitations are open.

Radically ordinary hospitality is reflected in Christian homes that resemble those of the first century. Such homes are communal.

They are deep and wide in Christian tradition and practice. As Christians we are a set-apart people, and we do things differently. We don't worry about what the unbelieving neighbors think, because the unbelieving neighbors are right here sharing our table, and they are more than happy to tell us what they think.

Practicing radically ordinary hospitality necessitates building margin time into the day, time where regular routines can be disrupted but not destroyed. This margin stays open for the Lord to fill—to take an older neighbor to the doctor, to babysit on the fly, to make room for a family displaced by a flood or a worldwide refugee crisis.

Living out radically ordinary hospitality leaves us with plenty to share, because we intentionally live below our means.

In radically ordinary hospitality, host and guest are interchangeable. If you come to my house for dinner and notice that I am still teaching a math lesson to a child, and my laundry remains on the dining room table unfolded, you roll up your sleeves and fold my laundry. Or set the table. Or load the dishwasher. Or feed the dogs. Radically ordinary hospitality means that hosts are not embarrassed to receive help, and guests know that their help is needed. A family of God gathering daily together needs each and every person. Host and guest are permeable roles.

Radically ordinary hospitality lived out in the family of God gathers daily, prays constantly, and needs no invitation to do so. And those who don't yet know the Lord are summoned for food and fellowship. Earthly good is shown as good, and the solitary may choose to be alone but need not be chronically lonely.

We practice radically ordinary hospitality by bearing sacrifices of obedience that God's people are called to offer. We don't think we are more merciful than God, so we don't encourage people to sin against him or violate what the Word of God says. We lament. We soberly know that God calls us to bear heavy and hard crosses, self-denials that feel like death. We trust God's power more than we trust our limitations, and we know that he never gives a command without giving the grace to perform it. But we know that the struggle is insurmountable alone. When radically ordinary hospitality is lived out, members of God's household are told that they are not alone in their struggles or their joys. Radically ordinary hospitality is accompanied by suffering.

Radically ordinary hospitality characterizes those who don't fuss over different worldviews represented at the dinner table. The truly hospitable aren't embarrassed to keep friendships with people who are different. They don't buy the world's bunk about this. They know that there is a difference between acceptance and approval, and they courageously accept and respect people who think differently from them. They don't worry that others will misinterpret their friendship. Jesus dined with sinners, but he didn't sin with sinners. Jesus lived in the world, but he didn't live like the world. This is the Jesus paradox. And it defines those who are willing to suffer with others for the sake of gospel sharing and gospel living, those who care more for integrity than appearances.

Engaging in radically ordinary hospitality means we provide the time necessary to build strong relationships with people who think differently than we do as well as build strong relationships from within the family of God. It means we know that only hypocrites and cowards let their words be stronger than their relationships, making sneaky raids into culture on social media or behaving like moralizing social prigs in the neighborhood. Radically ordinary hospitality shows this skeptical, post-Christian world what authentic Christianity looks like.

Radically ordinary hospitality gives evidence of faith in Jesus's power to save. It doesn't get dug in over politics or culture or where someone stands on current events. It knows what conversion means, what identity in Christ does, and what repentance creates. It knows that sin is deceptive. To be deceived means to be taken captive by an evil force to do its bidding. It knows that people need to be rescued from their sin, not to be given pep talks about good choice making. It remembers that Jesus rescues people from their sin. Jesus rescued us. Jesus lives and reigns. Radical hospitality shines through those who are no longer enslaved by the sin that once beckoned and bound them, wrapping its allegiance around their throat, even though old sins still know their name and address.

In the pages that follow, you are invited into my home, into my childhood, into my Bible reading, into my repentance, and into my homeschool schedules, shopping lists, simple meals, and daily, messy table fellowship. You will meet my family, my parents, my children, my neighbors, my enemies, and my friends.

If Mary Magdalene had written a book about hospitality for this post-Christian world, it would read like this one.

My prayer is that this book will help you let God use your home, apartment, dorm room, front yard, community gymnasium, or garden for the purpose of making strangers into neighbors and neighbors into family. Because that is the point—building the church and living like a family, the family of God. My prayer is that you will stop being afraid of strangers, even when some strangers are dangerous. My prayer is that you will grow to be more like Christ in practicing daily, ordinary, radical hospitality, and that the Lord would bless you richly for it, adding to his kingdom, creating a new culture and a new reputation for what it means to be a Christian to the watching world. My hope is that daily fellowship would grow your union with Christ and that you would no longer be that Christian with a pit of empty dreams competing madly with other reigning idols, wondering if this is all there is to the Christian life. My prayer is that you would see that practicing daily, ordinary, radical hospitality toward the end of rendering strangers neighbors and neighbors family of God is the missing link.

If this happens, then my prayer will be answered.

Priceless

The Merit of Hospitality

May 12, 2016, 5:15 a.m., Durham, North Carolina

A text message from a neighbor came in: "What's going on at Hank's house?[1] Why r police surrounding the house? R u OK?" But my phone was turned off and in the other room, so I didn't get the message.

Peaceful sleep sounds echoed from my husband and two youngest children. Even the dogs were sleeping. My Bible was open, along with my copy of *Tabletalk* magazine and my notebook. My coffee cup was in arm's reach, sitting on a calico mug mat that my ten-year-old daughter made in sewing class. Caspian, the enormous orange tabby, was sprawled over the table, under the hedonistic, narcotic bliss of a hastily consumed can of Fancy Feast Mixed Grill. I started my devotions that morning as I have been doing for the past seventeen years and as Ken and Floy Smith modeled for me: praying that the Lord would open my eyes to see wondrous things in his Word.

That morning, after I read through five psalms and one proverb,

I began to pray. I typically intersperse prayer with Bible reading and note taking. In the morning, I pray in concentric circles. I start by praying for myself, that the Lord would increase my love for him, grow me in holiness, give me courage to proclaim Christ in word and deed as a living epistle, lead me to repent, and give me the humble mind and heart of Christ and the kind comfort of the Holy Spirit to make me a more faithful and loving wife and mother and friend. I then pray for my family, the church, my neighbors, my nation, foreign missionaries, and missions. I thank the Lord that he is risen, that he prays for me, and that he has sent people into my life, starting with the Smiths, to bring me to himself and to hold me safely close. I thank God for the covenant, of which I am a part. I keep my prayer notebook open, and I flip through the pages as I pray through the names.

That morning, my prayer time stopped at the concentric circle labeled "neighbor." I was praying for my immediate neighbor, whose house I could see from my writing desk. I have always had a special affinity for front-door neighbors. Renee, Julie, Eddie, and now Hank. I love waking up and seeing the familiar van parked in the same spot, and as the sky yawns open, the house and people in it unveil their morning rituals (lights on, dogs out, paper retrieved, a wave of greeting, maybe a child running across the street to return a Tupperware or deliver a loose bouquet of red peonies). Loving your neighbors brings comfort and peace.

So there I was, praying for my neighbor. A typical morning. Except that the phone I had turned off, which was in the other room, continued to receive text messages alerting me that something was terribly, dreadfully wrong in the house across the street. The house of the man for whom I was praying.

———

Our house and Hank's house share a dead end that stops where two acres of woods open up. When Hank's moving van first backed down his driveway in 2014, he was a self-described recluse. He worked in his yard digging ditches—arbitrary and perfectly round holes that delighted my children because of their cookie-cutter symmetry and the very cool black snakes Hank unearthed and shared with them. He played loud music. He occasionally received cell phone calls that got him seething mad and shouting obscenities. He owned a one-hundred-pound pit bull named Tank who ran the streets without collar or tags. Each neighbor can recall how we all saw our life flash before our eyes the first time we met Tank, bounding toward us at full throttle. Hank didn't cut his grass for three months, and by the time the city fined him for creating a meadow, no regular mower could tackle the cleanup.

Truth be told, Hank was not the neighbor we had prayerfully asked for when Eddie sold the house and moved her family to Wisconsin. But we trusted that Hank was the neighbor God had planned for us. Good neighboring is at the heart of the gospel we know. So when Hank moved in, we shared with him our contact information, introduced him to our dogs and kids, and waited for him to reciprocate.

Instead, he dismantled his front doorbell so that no one else could disturb him.

We prayed for Hank.

We gently rebuked other neighbors for being suspicious or unkind in their questions and concerns about his reclusiveness.

For a year, it was like living across the street from Boo Radley, the misunderstood and demonized character in *To Kill a Mockingbird*.

And then one day Tank ran away and did not come home. One night turned into two, and two nights turned into a week. In the crisis of a lost dog—one who was also the closest companion of a lonely man—our bond was forged. We offered our help, and Hank received our open hand. We posted Tank's information on neighborhood listservs and enlisted other neighbors to come to Hank's aid. My ten-year-old daughter cried herself to sleep each night as she prayed for Tank's return, and she told Mr. Hank about her prayers and God's faithfulness.

When Tank was finally found safe and sound, we became friends. We started to walk our dogs together. Soon, we were eating meals together, spending holidays at our table, and sharing life. We learned that Hank lived alone, had severe clinical depression, PTSD, ADHD, and social anxiety.

Hank loved the woods as much as the children and I do. As winter opened into spring, we kept tally of our nesting red-shouldered hawks, our calling American toads, our migrating and returning robins, blue jays, woodpeckers, towhees, and ambling box turtles. Hank helped us chop down our dead trees and stack our wood. In his garage he always had the knick-knack one might need: a small flashlight to attach to a reflector vest for a night run, a hook that could hold doggie bags to the leash.

Hank was uneven. His depression made him so. Sometimes he stayed secluded in his home for weeks on end. We'd text and offer to help but to no avail. The only sign of life was that his garbage can would appear at the curb on the appointed night.

———

As neighbors were texting my turned-off phone about danger at Hank's house, I was sitting at my desk, praying for Hank.

I was praying for Hank's salvation.

And then I noticed it: burly men ducking around the back of my house, wearing orange shirts marked DEA—Drug Enforcement Agency. Serene darkness exploded with the unnatural intrusion of police lights. Yellow tape appeared everywhere—"Crime Scene." I left my Bible open to Psalm 42 and ran to wake Kent and the children. I grabbed my phone and turned it on. The text messages bounced into life: "What's going on at Hank's house? I hear there is a meth lab across the street from you!"

What does the conservative, Bible-believing family who lives across the street do in a crisis of this magnitude? How ought we to think about this? How ought we to live?

We could barrack ourselves in the house, remind ourselves and our children that "evil company perverts" (see 1 Cor. 15:33), and, like the good Pharisees that we are always poised to become, thank God that we are not like evil meth addicts.

We could surround our home in our own version of yellow crime-scene tape, giving the message that we are better than this, that we make good choices, that we would never fall into this mess.

We could surround ourselves with fear: What if the meth lab explodes and takes out my daughter's bedroom (the room closest to the lab) with it?

We could berate ourselves with criticism: How could we have allowed this meth addict into our hearts and our home?

But that, of course, is not what Jesus calls us to do.

As neighbors filed into our front yard, which had become front-row seats for an unfolding drama of epic magnitude, I scrambled eggs, put on a big pot of coffee, set out Bibles, and invited them in. Who else but Bible-believing Christians can make redemptive sense of tragedy? Who can see hope in the promises of God when the real, lived circumstances look dire? Who else knows that the sin that will undo me is my own, not my neighbor's, no matter how big my neighbor's sin may appear?

And where else but a Christian home should neighbors go in times of unprecedented crisis? Where else is it safe to be vulnerable, scared, lost, hopeless?

How else could we teach our children how to apply faith to the facts of life, a process that cancels out neither reality as it begs Jesus for hope, help, redemptive purpose, and saving grace? If we were to close the shades and numb ourselves through media intake or go into remote monologues about how we always knew he was bad, or how we always make good choices, what legacy would that leave to our children? Here is the thing about soothing yourself with self-delusion: no one buys it but you.

I had other things on my list of things to do that day but none more important than what I was doing. Gathering in distraught neighbors. Praying for my friend Hank.

Quickly and organically, our house became an all-day crisis station.

Neighbors—from children to the aged—who did not have to report to school or work stayed the day with us.

2

The Jesus Paradox

The Vitality of Hospitality

March 5, 2009, Fairfax, Virginia

It is a day before our new son's sixteenth birthday, and my husband, Kent, and I are about to meet him.

We stand at a precipice both familiar and foreign. Familiar, because we have already adopted three children. Familiar, because one of our children was also a teenager when we met her, and we know (or we think we do) what to expect. Foreign, because as committed pro-life Christians we know this: each life is a gift, each life is a mystery, each life reflects God's image, each life holds treasures indescribable, some of which take on the form of holes in your walls.

The current living situation of the son-we-have-not-yet-met is what polite company refers to as a "therapeutic group home," located about an hour from ours. After Kent returns home from work, we put Mary (age three) and Knox (age six) in their car seats and head off. We feel as though we are walking off a cliff. This is the most important endeavor, the most sacred risk, and the clearest picture of God's covenant I know of.

We enter a house that looks like any other, except the people inside are strangers to each other. The neat rows of children's shoes that wrap around the outside porch, ranging from very small to very large, reveal that the house is at full capacity. We are warmly welcomed to enter by one of the live-in social workers, and we are directed to sit in a formal living room, heavily reeking of white vinegar and pine room freshener.

None of the bedrooms have doors. Alarms ring upstairs as children with monitors on their ankles set off buzzers when they move from place to place, creating an anxious choir, exposing movement with no escape in sight.

No one is allowed outside.

Everyone is supervised all the time.

Children must seek permission to use the bathroom.

The rule charts on the kitchen walls are endless and daunting. Each child has his own neatly typed list, but they all begin like this: "Rise at five thirty, make bed, take medicine." The rule charts pour over the kitchen walls and into the hallway, creating a gothic paisley pattern, *The Yellow Wallpaper* style that forebodes unending potential failure, or madness, just like the heroine of Charlotte Perkins Gilman's turn-of-the-century novella of this title.

In the six-thousand-word feminist classic, *The Yellow Wallpaper*, the narrator slowly descends into madness, attributing the wallpaper as the source of her mental demise. The wallpaper's paisley yellow detail, like the ten-point rule charts in this group foster home, covers every base. Rule charts in these group homes record as a goal what the state envisions to be the best course of action for the child. Each child's "goal" is listed on the chart before the word "breakfast." The options include: reunification with birth family, adoption, or permanent foster care. Goals depend on either people who have already shown themselves to be undependable or strangers whose prospects are suspicious at best. Reunification with birth parents and adoption are such high-risk endeavors—so few teenagers realize either end point—that it feels hopeless to hope, not knowing if the next day will be a new nightmare or a rerun of an old nightmare.

I look at the charts and can't wrap my mind around how they can be successfully accomplished. It seems to me that no human being could possibly fulfill the expectations on these rule charts. It seems that creativity of any kind is the great enemy of self-control.

But these children have become robots.

They take medication to wake up, to focus on school, to remain calm on the interminable bus ride home, and to go to sleep.

They take medicine to forget the past, to remember the math lesson, and to separate themselves from more shattered hope, names to unlearn, memories to flush, a future that slips between fingers.

I want to like the house and the foster parents that run it.

I want to see them in me and me in them.

But this is no home.

This is prison.

And this is one of the finest government-run therapeutic foster homes in one of the wealthiest counties in the United States.

The social worker who runs the house repeats the need to maintain strict rules and regular medication. Our son Knox has brought a present for Michael: an olive-green, plastic triceratops with a foot chewed off, thanks to our golden retriever, Sally. It occurs to me, as I look at the mauled plastic dinosaur, that there are no visible toys in this house. Not one errant Lego or escaped Matchbox car. No clutter.

Let me say right off that I know rules are important. The first question every foster child able to speak asked me upon entering our house was this: "What are the rules?" I know that sin reigns in the heart of man. I know that we are born sinners, that "behold, I was brought forth in iniquity, and in sin did my mother conceive me" (Ps. 51:5). I know that sin resides in our patterns, even our patterns of survival.

But this house disturbs me. On the wall are tapestry samplers that display pastel and cursive quilting: "Home Sweet Home." In the bedrooms are wards of the state, medicated to the hilt, needing permission to use the bathroom.

I know that I can be deluded.

I know that many foster moms, in pride, think, "I can do better than this. My love is bigger than this. I can save this child."

But that's not where I'm going with this.

I know I can't save anyone. Jesus alone saves, and all I do is show up.

Show up we must.

And now, having shown up, I can tell you that this house gives me the creeps.

Numbers go through my head when I am threatened. Now, I think about the seven thousand teenagers who "age out" of foster care and who often end up in prison or homeless or dead. I know that this house is better than prison or homeless or dead. But still. I ponder the 105,000 children in foster care nationwide, waiting for nightmares to end. I sit here in this house, in my class and racial privilege, and I know what it means to pray for the whole lost world of mankind, myself being the chief of sinners, pleading with God to undo me so that I can do good to everyone (Gal. 6:10), so I can honor and respect all (1 Pet. 2:17).

Mrs. Jones brings Michael to us, and I behold one of the most beautiful children I have ever seen. All legs and pimples, he towers over me, long Afro, mild-brown eyes, and caramel-candy complexion. And he is scared. He looks right past me and fixes his gaze on Knox and Mary. He gets down on the floor with them, at eye level. The world stands still, and then suddenly his face lights up with joy. Mary gives him a hug, and Knox gives him a mauled army-green dinosaur. This looks like a family reunion, except that we are all strangers.

Michael jumps up and begs the supervisor to let him please, please, please return to his room to get his family picture. He is talking a mile a minute, and his whole body is gyrating in place. He just must have it to show to this boy here, this Knox boy. This Knox boy must see his family. His brothers. He pleads. He wheels around. He ticks. He won't stop. She relents.

Moments later Michael returns with something cupped protectively in his hands. A Polaroid picture, lined with tears and sweaty hands, the corners curling in. It is the only remnant of proof that Michael survived another life in another world, with unfinished business in that past world that dogs him. There were good things too, and they call his name, and they are trapped with him in the picture. He is a boy stuck. He can't get back to this Polaroid world, and without the Polaroid world, he can't take up residence in this one. Every child I have ever known who spent time in foster care has a picture like this, with a trap door almost impossible to unhinge.

Michael flashes the picture before my and Kent's eyes briefly and then settles back down on the floor with the children, cupping his hands protectively around this treasure. With his Polaroid in his hands, he no longer gyrates. He breathes deeply. Heavily.

Knox and Mary know that this is a sacred moment, and they wait for Michael to reveal the treasure in his cupped hand. They are expecting him to reveal a just-captured toad or a chocolate kiss.

When no toad or chocolate kiss appears, they seem to have an uncanny sense not to appear disappointed. Of course, they don't know how to interpret the old picture of three children, one with a bushy Afro, the other with a missing front tooth, the smallest one with a faraway look just like the one Knox always seems to have on his face when the camera flashes. The faraway-look boy is wearing a Thomas the Tank Engine T-shirt and holding a beige stuffed bear with a red tartan bow. The boy in the picture looks strikingly like both of the boys in the room, my son(s), one whom I have known for six years and the other whom I have known for a few minutes. From that moment on, I had twin boys separated by a decade.

Michael says, "This is a picture of my brother, Aaron."

Knox says, "I know that is me, but I don't have that Thomas shirt!"

I know that is me. No this is a picture of my brother. Other brother, not you, brother. Your brother is me. I am your brother. You are my brother, and this is me.

The mystery of the covenant of family unfolds in places like this, with majesty and miracle on display, and in the background the dim thudding of alarm bells that demarcate a child unfairly deemed juvenile delinquent getting permission to leave his room and use the bathroom.

In all my years of parenting, and with all the children I have held, comforted, fed, tucked in, listened to, and prayed for, nothing has prepared me for this moment. For reasons that I cannot explain and that no parenting book has ever explained, my identity as a mom comes into full view when faced with a frightened, angry, misunderstood teenager. I love them instantly. No parenting book, no conversation with experienced parents, and no life experience prepared me for what it means to love at first sight my newly met son: a courageous boy, gangly and awkward, who stands a foot taller than I do.

Teenagers placed in foster care feel broken and unwanted. They have told me that they feel like lepers. They need the Advocate, Jesus himself. Often they feel marked and shamed. Outsiders. Rejects. Even the rules of the system work against them. They need grace. We need grace. Contagious grace.

————

When Jesus walked the earth, leprosy was the worst of all plagues. Not only was it a filthy, deadly disease from which no one recovered, but its contagion spread arbitrarily and wildly, rendering beloved family members outcasts and wanderers in the beat of a heart. Like Frankenstein's creature, the leper's skin no longer covered his sinews and muscles. With a pop of white pus, a beloved family member overnight became abhorrent. Lepers—moral and social outcasts, isolated, rejected, feared, despised—banded together in pain, waiting to die, bereft of hope. Leprosy was a medical plague with legal warrants for arrest and disbandment. The ceremonial law deemed the leper morally and physically unclean. Leprosy was more than an infectious skin disease. It rendered the person who embodied it unfit to be part of a healthy community and unable to join in the worship of God. When Jesus walked the earth, leprosy was thus a repulsive *corporealization* of original sin. It was not caused by a particular sin or behavior. Rather, it pointed to our sin nature, the walking time bomb inside each and every one of us. The only solution was containment of the leper and protection for the yet healthy. Whole chapters of the law—Leviticus 13 and 14— are devoted to how to contain the contagion and restore the healed leper. This disease could transform a beloved father or mother into a despised outcast overnight. One day you could enjoy belonging, touch, recognition, value. The next, you were as good as garbage.

Leprosy was no metaphor.

It was real as rain.

And when God sent his son, Jesus, fully God and fully man, to live on earth, two remarkable things happened.

Luke 5 records how a man "full of leprosy" walked up to Jesus. Let's stop right there. Jesus was not visiting a leper colony in this particular scene. He was not going to the outcast, out to the margins. No, here the margins were moving to the center. The leper left the leper colony (illegal, dangerous for all parties) and made a beeline for Jesus and fell on his face. The man with leprosy begged, "Lord, if you will, you can make me clean" (Luke 5:12). It took mountain-moving faith and courage—perhaps even prophetic faith and courage—to leave the leper colony and head to the heart of the city, to leave the safety of one's culture, one's people, one's appointed place, and go to Jesus. As he approached Jesus, his mind must have been swirling with self-condemnation: *You are a danger to yourself and others; you are breaking the law; you will hurt those you love*. But his faith carried him with courage. And we know that faith compelled this man, because he called Jesus "Lord"—a title for Jesus that only the faithful in Scripture used. Faith in Jesus made the leper do the unthinkable. The leper risked arrest. The leper risked causing a public health crisis and infecting others. The leper risked a potential mob driving him away, returning him to face the facts squarely: he was damaged goods, with no hope apart from Christ.

And the leper was a better image bearer than we.

He knew he was damaged goods.

The leper knew he needed Jesus, not social betterment.

And then Jesus did the craziest thing anyone had ever seen.

He touched this man—the man who had not been touched since the plague had ravaged his body, the man whose fate was sealed from the moment the first white sore appeared. This very same man was touched by the Son of God.

"And Jesus stretched out his hand and touched him, saying, 'I will; be clean'" (Luke 5:13).

That touch changed the man. But the touch did more than that. That touch changed the world.

When Jesus touched the leper, he did not invent grace. God the Father did, and we see this throughout the Old Testament, even in healing leprosy. The great Syrian general Naaman was healed of his leprosy by Elisha, thanks to the spiritual wisdom of a nameless Hebrew slave girl who knew above all else that there is a prophet in Israel who heals (2 Kings 5:1–14). Luke records how important Naaman's healing was: "And there were many lepers in Israel in the time of the prophet Elisha, and none of them was cleansed, but only Naaman the Syrian" (Luke 4:27). I suspect Elisha healed Naaman for the sake of the nameless Hebrew slave, whose faith was strong and more contagious than the leprosy of her master. Indeed, she had faith that Elisha could do something that he had never done before. Because that is what real faith is: resting in assurance on a promise of God that has yet to be materialized.

It is vital to see what healing and salvation mean when they come from the hand of God.

It is vital to have the eyes to see what Jesus did.

It is also vital to see what Jesus did not do.

He did not tell the leper that God loved and approved of him just as he was. Jesus did not say that the problem of leprosy was a social construction rooted only in the mind of the beholder, and now that "grace" had arrived, "the law" was no longer binding. Jesus did not encourage the leper to develop greater self-esteem. Nor did Jesus rebuke the faith community for upholding irrational taboos against leprosy—leprophobia. No. The problem was the contagion, and the contagion was no social construct. The contagion was dangerous.

When Jesus walked the earth, he wasn't afraid to touch hurting people.

He drew people in close.

He met them empty and left them full.

Jesus turned everything upside down.

This is the Jesus paradox—the touch from Jesus that launches a contagion of grace for those who believe, repent, turn, and follow, a contagion of grace that allows the believer to love those who hate in return and to pray, serve, and sacrifice so that others, like the nameless Hebrew slave, can know that God is alive and rescues those who call.

Jesus can set into motion a contagion of grace with his touch because the Son of God has fulfilled the law of God and has mercy on his people, knowing that we are sinners, mere men and women, unable to save ourselves. Jesus came untouched by the original sin that distorts, the actual sin that distracts, and the indwelling sin that manipulates. Jesus is no puppet on the strings of Satan, as we too often are. And when Jesus fulfilled the law by dying on the cross and rising by his own power to sit at God the Father's right hand, he gave his people the power to overcome the sin that enslaves them. He gave us his blood to wash away our sins, he gave us his Word to instruct and heal us, and he sent the Holy Spirit to lead us in conviction and repentance of sin and to comfort us by the assurance that his saving love is rock solid. He gave us our inheritance as adopted children of Almighty God.

But he did not leave us there, little isolated agents of grace, running our own "random acts of kindness" campaign. No, he gave us his bride, the church—his church—to which we who believe are called to make a covenant of membership, to become a family, to be both set apart from and missionally placed in the world, to take care in a daily way of our brothers and sisters in Christ, to receive instruction and rebuke when needed, to support the pastor and elders in church discipline, to act like a visible family of God, and to draw others who do not yet know the pricey love of God into our homes, families, and churches.

The Jesus paradox manifests contagious grace as practiced by ordinary people like me and you, desperately needed, especially now, in our post-Christian world.

But how do we as Christians live in contagious grace?

To see that in action, let's move to the Gospel of John, to witness the first miracle of Jesus, turning mere water into wine at the wedding in Cana. Here, Jesus models contagious grace through a hospitality so radical, so undeniable, that a common wedding in a piddling, insignificant village becomes host to a miracle, a miracle that takes us from empty to full.[1] The key to contagious grace—the grace that allows the margins to move to the center, the grace that commands you to never fear the future, the grace that reveals that what humbles you cannot hurt you if Jesus is your Lord—that grace is ours when we do what Mary says to do in this scene. She says to the servants (and the Holy Spirit says to us): "Do whatever he tells you" (John 2:5).

Simple, right? No. We cannot will ourselves into the deep obedience that God requires. We can't obey until we ourselves have received this grace and picked up our cross. We can't obey until we have laid down our life, with all our false and worldly identities and idols. We can't obey until we face the facts: the gospel comes in exchange for the life we once loved. But when we die to ourselves, we find the liberty to obey. As Susan Hunt explains, "When God's grace changes our status from rebel to redeemed, we are empowered by his Spirit to obey him. We are transformed by the renewing of our minds (Rom. 12:2) into his likeness (2 Cor. 3:18). Joyful obedience is the evidence of our love for Jesus (John 14:15)."[2]

When we receive God's saving grace, can we do this? Can we give until it hurts? Yes, because God tells us that we are strong: "I write to you, young men, because you are strong, and the word of God abides in you, and you have overcome the evil one" (1 John 2:14). We are stronger than we think. Even in our struggle against sin, God tells us that we, his children, are strong.

Obedience to Jesus—dying to self, doing whatever he wants in spite of the cravings of our flesh—renders liberty, with arms open wide, with bread and fish to give away, with a shocking recognition for the outcast and despised, remembering that we were once her. This was true when Jesus walked the earth, and it is true today, in our post-Christian world, where the Christian faith is dismissed or despised and where Christian values are seen as the enemy of compassion, care, and diversity.

What Is Radically Ordinary Hospitality?

Radically ordinary hospitality is this: using your Christian home in a daily way that seeks to make strangers neighbors, and neighbors family of God. It brings glory to God, serves others, and lives out the gospel in word and deed. If you are prohibited from using your living space in this way, it counts if you support in some way some household in your church that is doing it. The purpose of radically ordinary hospitality is to build, focus, deepen, and strengthen the family of God, pointing others to the Bible-believing local church, and being earthly and spiritual good to everyone we know.

When our Christian homes are open, we make transparent to a watching world what Christ is doing with our bodies, our families, and our world. When we daily gather with family of God in organic and open and communal ways and invite those who do not yet know Christ to enter, we accompany one another in suffering. We bear one another's burdens. We show a watching world what fervent prayer sounds like—talking to God, knowing that we are, through the merits of Christ, on good terms with him, and that our daily needs are his concern. When our Christian homes are open, our unsaved neighbors watch us struggle with our own sins—both the sins of our doing and the sin nature with which we wage daily combat.

For Christians to maintain an authentic Christian witness to a world that mistrusts us (at the very least), we must be transparently hospitable. The Christian life is a cross-bearing life, and the Word of God calls and equips God's people to holy living. All our neighbors must know that we live differently from the world, and they will know as we live visibly within the means of grace, placing ourselves under the authority of the church as members in good standing—and we must be unmistakably hospitable.

First, we must live under the authority of God and church if we are to call others to live differently. We must be active, tithing members of a Bible-believing church, under her covenant of church membership, and willing to receive instruction and rebuke if needed. We must be teachable. We have no business calling our neighbors to live differently if we don't.

Second, we must work hard to know who our neighbors are and how they struggle. We want to show respect and a helping hand. Christians often misunderstand this. Often, Christians ask me, "How can I love my neighbor without misleading her into thinking I approve of everything she does?" First, remember that Christians cannot give good answers to bad questions. No one approves of everything that others do. No one. It is a false question. The better question is this: "How can my neighbors know that because I live under God's authority rather than the compulsions of my own selfish desires, their secrets are safe with me?" The answer is simple: love the sinner and hate your own sin. Or, as Mark says, "Have salt in yourselves, and be at peace with one another" (Mark 9:50).

Radically ordinary hospitality may resemble the social-gospel practices of liberal churches and non-Christian mercy communities, for radically ordinary hospitality engages in some of the same practices: we gather people in close, we feed and clothe the poor, we accept people where they are, we care for the needs of the body, and we seek to restore the dignity of each human being. But here is the big difference: radically ordinary hospitality practiced by biblical Christians views struggling people as image bearers of a holy God, needing faith in Christ alone, belief in Jesus the rescuer of his people, repentance of sin, and covenant family within the church. Bible-believing Christians do not believe that a shave and a meal help people in the long run—or atone for the sin nature of us all.

Strangers and refugees are marked by the dignity of the God of the universe but also by the imputation of Adam's sin. In order for the gospel to be proclaimed in deed and word, we must recognize that we all deserve hell itself—with all its ravages, injustices, poverty, and pain—and that only through the blood of Christ, poured out for the sins of his people, and through the power that God used to raise Christ from the grave, bestowed upon all who submit to the authority of Scripture, are any of us saved. The Christian home is the place where we bring the church to the people as we seek to lock arms together.

Christian hospitality violates the usual boundary maintenance enacted by table fellowship. When I was in graduate school, we all devoured books by the cultural anthropologist Mary Douglas. Her book *Purity and Danger: An Analysis of Concepts of Pollution and Taboo* was formative to my thinking about insiders and outsiders, belonging and rejection, and the boundaries to our homes and *habitus*—norms, dispositions, capacities, and propensities that make up our heart and home and community.[3]

Douglas's essay "Deciphering a Meal" was instrumental in developing the radical hospitality that knit the lesbian and gay community together during the confusing and terrifying 1980s and 1990s, when AIDS was called "gay cancer" and when people who identified as gay were believed to be carriers of a plague.[4] Douglas explains how meals provide boundary maintenance between people who share different cultural norms and how dietary laws police the "social body." I have always loved this essay. But it was only years later, as a Christian, that I could see how identity politics divides people. Table fellowship that depends on identity sameness banks on a false understanding of personhood.

God declares our identity: we are male or female image bearers of a holy God, with a soul that will last forever and a gendered body that, for those who have put their hope in Jesus, in faith and repentance, will be glorified and embodied in the New Jerusalem after Jesus returns. Conversely, identity politics depends on the idea that the social body is preeminent—that we are primarily and powerfully a member of a body politic first, and only secondarily a private citizen.[5] As a Christian, this has become revolutionary to my thinking about hospitality. It means that exclusion of people for arbitrary reasons—not church discipline–related ones (an important exception I discuss in chapter 6)—is violent and hostile. It kills faith and discourages believers and contradicts the clear message of the Bible: God's people were strangers once. We know where it hurts.

I think about Mary Douglas a lot these days, as table fellowship is a daily way of life for me.

Kent and I practice daily hospitality as a way of life because we must. We remember what it is like to be lonely. We remember the odd contradiction: to be told on the Lord's Day that you are part of the family of God but then to limp along throughout the rest of the long week like an orphan begging bread. We know that chronic loneliness can kill people and destroy their hope and faith. We believe that the Bible's high calling for singleness compels us to live communally when we can and to feast nightly on meals and Scripture and prayer with doors wide open. Fasting, a discipline of the faith, is best broken with a communal meal and prayer. We believe that the blood of Christ is thicker than the blood of water. Daily hospitality, gathering church and neighbors, is a daily grace.

And we believe that radically ordinary hospitality depends on the family of God knowing where to gather, knowing how to be organic and spontaneous with Scripture and open arms. And we do it because the purpose of radically ordinary hospitality is to take the hand of a stranger and put it in the hand of the Savior, to bridge hostile worlds, and to add to the family of God.

So we, the well-known conservative Christians on the block, run a house that from the outside looks like a Christian commune. And we do not believe that this is excessive. We believe this is what the Bible calls *normal*. We believe that Christians are called to live as the family of God and to draw strangers and neighbors in, with food and a bended knee, beseeching God's grace to pour out on those who do not yet know the Lord and to encourage and uplift and fuel those who do. We lock arms together because we must. Christians are not lone rangers.

And, yes, daily hospitality can be expensive and even inconvenient. It compels us to care more for our church family and neighbors than our personal status in this world. Our monthly grocery bill alone reminds us that what humbles us cannot hurt us, but what puffs up our pride unwaveringly will.

Living out radically ordinary Christian hospitality means knowing that your relationship with others must be as strong as your words. The balance cannot tip here. Having strong words and a weak relationship with your neighbor is violent. It captures the violent carelessness of our social media–infused age. That is not how neighbors talk with each other. That is not how image bearers of the same God relate to one another. Radically ordinary hospitality values the time it takes to invest in relationships, to build bridges, to repent of sins of the past, to reconcile. Bridge building and remaking friendships cannot be rushed.

The word *hospitality* approximates the Greek word *philoxenia*, which means "love of the stranger." Instead of feeling sidelined by the sucker punches of post-Christianity, Christians are called to practice radically ordinary hospitality to renew their resolve in Christ. Too many of us are sidelined by fears. We fear that people will hurt us. We fear that people will negatively influence our children. We fear that we do not even understand the language of this new world order, least of all its people. We long for days gone by. Our sentimentality makes us stupid. We need to snap ourselves out of this self-pitying reverie. The best days are ahead. Jesus advances from the front of the line.

Radically ordinary hospitality can indeed be used by the Lord to grow his people in grace and sacrificial living, to preserve practices, ideas, and cultures that God has established for our blessing and his glory, to bring those in places of agonizing darkness into Christian homes and friendships, and, indeed, if God so wills, to change the world. But radically ordinary Christian hospitality must be rooted and steeped in grace: church membership, private prayer and fasting, solitude, repentance, Bible reading, Scripture memory, and worshipful singing.

Spiritual Preparations for Radically Ordinary Hospitality

Radically ordinary hospitality does not simply flow from the day-to-day interests of the household. You must prepare spiritually. The Bible calls spiritual preparation *warfare*. Radically ordinary hospitality is indeed spiritual warfare.

These ideas don't go together in polite society. Hospitality conjures up a scene of a Victorian tea, with crocheted doilies and China-inspired, blue and white, paisley-patterned teacups. *Radical* means "change from the root" and conjures up political and social upheaval and the kind of change that normally scares the pants off conservative Christians. *Ordinary* means "everyday," "common-place," "predictable," "reliable," and "regular." And spiritual warfare is what we engage in when temptation is clobbering us again, and Satan is winning, tearing us, our Christian witness, and our families apart. Only in the Jesus paradox do these incongruous ideas come together. And come together they must.

Radically Ordinary Hospitality

In my world, the fine china and the crocheted doilies are in boxes in the attic, swapped for sensible cotton and Corelle on most days, and sturdy Wedgwood plates and bowls paired with mismatched and flashy Fiesta-knockoff, ceramic glasses on others. My hospitality is practical, unfussy, and constant. Sometimes I play the posture of host, obeying God's commands, and sometimes I am in the role of guest, receiving nourishment and care. But we are always one or the other—we are either hosts, or we are guests. The Christian life makes no room for independent agents, onlookers, renters. We who are washed in the blood of Christ are stakeholders.

Ordinary hospitality works on the principle of tithing. God commands that we are either returning 10 percent of what he provides to us to our church or receiving aid from our church because we are in desperate need of help. Both giving and receiving bless the church. And if we aren't giving or receiving—tithes or hospitality—we are robbing God.

The same principle is true for hospitality. We must be willing to practice hospitality as both host and guest, and we must see how the principle of both giving and receiving builds a community and glorifies God. Again, there are no renters or onlookers or gawkers in the kingdom of God. We are hosts and guests together, and both generous giving and open receiving bless God.

God calls Christians to practice hospitality in order to build loving Christian communities, to build nightly table fellowship with fellow image bearers, to ease the pain of orphanhood, widowhood, and prison, to be qualified as elders in the church, and to be good and faithful stewards of what God has given to us in the person, work, example, obedience, and suffering of the Lord Jesus Christ. This gospel call that renders strangers into neighbors into family of God is all pretty straight up when you read the Bible, especially the book of Acts. And it requires both hosts and guests. We must participate as both hosts and guests—not just one or the other—as giving and receiving are good and sacred and connect people and communities in important ways.

But this is not where it ends. God calls us to practice hospitality as a daily way of life, not as an occasional activity when time and finance allow. Radically ordinary hospitality means this: God promises to put the lonely in families (Ps. 68:6), and he intends to use your house as living proof.

Spiritual Warfare

Radically ordinary hospitality creates an intimacy among people that allows for genuine differences to be discussed. Christians see this world as a host to cosmic struggles against the powers of evil and between the flesh and the spirit, as a place that we are called to make beautiful through gospel grace, as we live out these middle chapters of our lives. When I say that hospitality is spiritual warfare, please don't picture violence or angry shouting. The idea of spiritual warfare in the Bible refers to the process by which believers taste and see the power of the age to come every time they open their Bibles and every time they bring their petitions to the throne of grace in prayer. Spiritual warfare is the behind-the-scenes reality of what happens when we share the power of the resurrected Christ with our neighbors. Spiritual warfare is realistic, because evil lurks in the world and in the hearts of men. To engage in it is to beckon the reign of Christ to overcome evil as we seek to practice what we believe and thereby "overcome evil with good" (Rom. 12:21).

First, radically ordinary hospitality reflects that the words you speak reveal that you are owned by Christ. You are not a people pleaser. Even if you lose friendships for a season, your union with Christ is secure:

> I am sure that neither death nor life, nor angels nor rulers, nor things present nor things to come, nor powers, nor height nor depth, nor anything else in all creation, will be able to separate us from the love of God in Christ Jesus our Lord. (Rom. 8:38–39)

This passage lays bare that radically ordinary hospitality paves a way for deep union with Christ. Radically ordinary hospitality renews our faith and revives our hope.

Second, practicing radically ordinary hospitality sanctifies us by putting us in a sacrificial posture of service to others. It cautions us to think before we act. It might even become a life pattern for all future generations in your home:

> For you were called to freedom, brothers. Only do not use your freedom as an opportunity for the flesh, but through love serve one another. For the whole law is fulfilled in one word: "You shall love your neighbor as yourself." But if you bite and devour one another, watch out that you are not consumed by one another. But I say, walk by the Spirit, and you

will not gratify the desires of the flesh. For the desires of the flesh are against the Spirit, and the desires of the Spirit are against the flesh, for these are opposed to each other, to keep you from doing the things you want to do. But if you are led by the Spirit, you are not under the law. Now the works of the flesh are evident: sexual immorality, impurity, sensuality, idolatry, sorcery, enmity, strife, jealousy, fits of anger, rivalries, dissensions, divisions, envy, drunkenness, orgies, and things like these. I warn you, as I warned you before, that those who do such things will not inherit the kingdom of God. But the fruit of the Spirit is love, joy, peace, patience, kindness, goodness, faithfulness, gentleness, self-control; against such things there is no law. And those who belong to Christ Jesus have crucified the flesh with its passions and desires. If we live by the Spirit, let us also keep in step with the Spirit. Let us not become conceited, provoking one another, envying one another. (Gal. 5:13–26)

Third, radically ordinary hospitality is part of our spiritual armor, allowing us access to people's broken hearts, allowing the Spirit of God to work through us in spite of our limitations:

Finally, be strong in the Lord and in the strength of his might. Put on the whole armor of God, that you may be able to stand against the schemes of the devil. For we do not wrestle against flesh and blood, but against the rulers, against the authorities, against the cosmic powers over this present darkness, against the spiritual forces of evil in the heavenly places. Therefore take up the whole armor of God, that you may be able to withstand in the evil day, and having done all, to stand firm. Stand therefore, having fastened on the belt of truth, and having put on the breastplate of righteousness, and, as shoes for your feet, having put on the readiness given by the gospel of peace. In all circumstances take up the shield of faith, with which you can extinguish all the flaming darts of the evil one; and take the helmet of salvation, and the sword of the Spirit, which is the word of God. (Eph. 6:10–17)

Fourth, practicing radically ordinary hospitality gives us heavenly peers—the great cloud of witnesses:

> Therefore, since we are surrounded by so great a cloud of witnesses, let us also lay aside every weight, and sin which clings so closely, and let us run with endurance the race that is set before us. (Heb. 12:1).

We see Paul as our brother and role model who practiced radical hospitality in prison and who rightly understood that his chains made him bold. In Ephesians 6:20 Paul tells us that he is an "ambassador in chains" for the purpose of speaking boldly. Paul closes his letter to the Colossians by asking his readers to "remember my chains" (Col. 4:18). What chains do we bear? Do they make us bold? They ought to. The chains of our post-Christian world are meant to make us bold, not bashful. Selecting the great cloud of witnesses and Paul as our role models helps us steer clear of selfish cultural biases and influences, where prosperity compels some to value too highly the things of this world.

Practicing radically ordinary hospitality is your street credibility with your post-Christian neighbors. It allows you to listen, to keep secrets, to be a safe friend, and to speak a word of grace into dark places. In post-Christian communities, your words can be only as strong as your relationships. Your best weapon is an open door, a set table, a fresh pot of coffee, and a box of Kleenex for the tears that spill:

> For the weapons of our warfare are not of the flesh but have divine power to destroy strongholds. We destroy arguments and every lofty opinion raised against the knowledge of God, and take every thought captive to obey Christ, being ready to punish every disobedience, when your obedience is complete. (2 Cor. 10:4–6)

Understanding radically ordinary hospitality as a form of spiritual warfare also helps Christians be flexible with the roles they will assume. Christians must learn to practice radically ordinary hospitality not only as the hosts of this world but, perhaps more importantly, as its despised guests. Let's face it: we have become unwelcome guests in this post-Christian world. Our children ride their scooters in neighborhoods where conservative Christianity is dismissed or denounced as irrelevant, irrational, discriminatory, and dangerous. Many of us go to work in places where sensitivity training has become an Orwellian nightmare; where sexual orientation is now considered a true category of personhood (who you really are); where biological sex is no longer considered a factual reality, offering God's designed blessing for all of humanity, but only a psychological reality (its meaning subject to how you feel). Christian common sense is declared "hate speech" by the new keepers of this culture. The old rules don't apply anymore. Many Christians genuinely do not know what to say to their unbelieving neighbors. The language and the logic have changed almost overnight. The invitation to bring people who despise you into your home may sound like a horrific prospect.

One option is to build the walls higher, declare more vociferously that our homes are our castles, and, since the world is going to hell in a handbasket, we best get inside, thank God for the moat, and draw up the bridge. Doing so practices war on this world but not the kind of spiritual warfare that drives out darkness and brings in the kindness of the gospel. Strategic wall building serves only to condemn the world and the people in it. This kind of war betrays our faith as hollow, vapid, and powerless.

Our other option is to despise the blood of Christ and reinvent a Christianity that fits nicely on the "coexist" bumper sticker, avoiding the disgrace and shame of the cross for a respectable religion that bows to the idols of our day: consumerism and sexual autonomy. This manipulation strategy relies on using biblical words in anti-biblical ways. It shares with biblical Christianity the same vocabulary but not the same dictionary. This option is equally dreadful, and prevalent.

But—in order to practice radically ordinary hospitality as

spiritual warfare—we must be deep in the means of grace and fluent with the way that God's law and God's grace cannot be compromised or detached. Do we spend enough time within the boundaries of our Christian faith to renew, rebuild, recharge, repent, and grow in Christ—and to teach our children to understand that we are nonnative speakers in this new world culture? We must. We must build strong Christian infrastructures and launch from these.

By so doing, we take Paul at his word: "The weapons of our warfare are not of the flesh but have divine power to destroy strongholds" (2 Cor. 10:4).

But how? Deviled eggs with divine power? Muddy kid and dog footprints all over the house (especially on the cream-colored carpet) as heavenly proof that herein tromps the "feet of him who brings good news" (Isa. 52:7)?

No.

Instead, God calls us to make sacrifices that hurt so that others can be served and maybe even saved. We are called to die. Nothing less.

Radically ordinary hospitality serves ravioli with redemption life. It is fearless; it is faithful. As Russell Moore writes, describing another context for spiritual engagements with culture, it "doesn't blink before power, but doesn't seek to imitate it either."[6]

Where to start? I start with a list.

I am a list maker.

Latin vocabulary, books I want to read, people I need to write to, daily chores (mine and the children's), knitting projects, children's clothing and shoe sizes (constantly changing), food allergies of people I love, words of life to include in letters to my friends in prison, prayer requests, neighborhood children's birthdays and their favorite snacks, the names and personalities of the dogs that somehow end up in my backyard or sleeping on my couch. Sometimes these lists take the form of group text messages to the women in my neighborhood: "I'll be at Costco today after school. Text me your list and I'll drop off your things on my way home."

But usually my lists are made on steno pads, which I carry in my purse with my knitting project and my Bible and my wallet and pull out and leave on the kitchen counter next to the coffee pot when I'm home.

I don't use my iPhone for making lists.

If I did that, no one else could see them, and then no one else could get on board.

I like to do things by hand and by heart.

My hospitality list—the list that I work over throughout the week in the manner that I knead the Communion bread I make every Saturday night—includes my grocery lists and the grocery lists of my neighborhood friends and the meals I will be delivering and the people I anticipate serving that week. You see, not a day goes by when I do not think about hospitality and table fellowship—the lost Christian art of loving inclusion, the lost witness of what Christian family really means, and the lost lilting of a heart that breaks so that it can be remade by God. I pray the works of my hands and heart will shape a place where Jesus lays his head, as strangers and friends fill my table and hear the words of life as we break bread together.

My lists are reflective of my schedule, which looks like this:

Lord's Day. We are Sabbatarians, so we enjoy the whole day as set apart for worship and fellowship. I finish preparing food for our weekly fellowship meal at church and our home fellowship, which includes the meal in the evening for anywhere from ten to thirty people.

Monday. Mondays are hard days for homeschooling, so we end with friends coming over, and going on a long dog walk or bike ride. When we return, and while kids play outside, I sometimes put together and deliver a meal for a neighbor in need.

Tuesday. Homeschooling and piano lessons followed by dinner with our neighbors and church friends are the Tuesday routine, along with extended prayer time and Bible study because we are all struggling with something. These days we talk about the way that public policy squeezes Christianity into a false box we hardly recognize. I try to be ready for others to join us and prepare for ten, because Tuesday nights are turning into community prayer time as well.

Wednesday. More homeschooling on Wednesdays, and cleaning the house after school. Sometimes we run out to the local jail and put money in the commissary fund of a prisoner friend, Aimee, so that she can purchase a sweatshirt, as the nights are getting cooler, and detoxing from meth is awful. My children accompany me on this task because they accompany me in praying for our neighbors in prison. The day ends with prayer meeting at the church at seven o'clock.

Thursday. Thursdays bring more homeschooling and maybe a trip to the library or the local science museum if we finish by four o'clock. We participate in a seven o'clock prayer walk with neighbors if the weather is good. If the weather is bad, we meet for prayer in our living room. We have designated Thursday as "neighbor night" for years now, and new people regularly show up for prayer and fellowship.

Friday. This is homeschool co-op day. Sometimes I meet with other homeschool moms at noon to go over Latin grammar. We rebuild the ruins of our own minds with Latin. Latin grammar has become vital to me. It is concrete, not abstract. I need more things that are concrete these days. After school I plan a Costco trip for Friday night. Susanna and daughter Mary come too. Then we have a late dinner with neighbors and children, creating friendships that span worldview as we hear gales of laughter from a painting table in the homeschool room and from the trampoline out in the backyard.

Saturday. I may start the day with a morning dog walk with neighbors. Children (mine and those from the neighborhood) come and go as they build a fort in the backyard or assemble as The Council outside with light sabers and forts. At some point I make Communion bread and clean the house. Sometimes I enjoy a visit with my oldest son and daughter-in-law and grandson. In the evening we gather with church members and neighbors who want to prepare for the Lord's Day with a meal and prayer.

My lists are not set in stone; they are set in grace, organized around people and their needs and their special pain and deep wounds and unbearable secrets. Some of my lists look like common grocery lists, but that is only if you see the surface of things. Committing your life to good neighboring is both art and science. I've always been a specialist. My specialty is repentance and solitude, with food and faith combined, and family of God always in the mind's eye of God's making. My special move these days involves dying a thousand deaths daily for the love of God and neighbor.

The upshot of all these lists is that, after dinner, the Bible and the Psalters are opened and Kent teaches, and we—a shabby, makeshift "we" of a people, neighbors and God's family all tossed together in a heap—listen, question, weep, sing, laugh, receive, and pray. Jesus enters the conversation, not to shut down opposition, but to shape it, to pry us open to light. All these lists lead to this moment, when strangers are rendered brothers and sisters in Christ, heads bowed; when the Holy Spirit drives, Jesus speaks, and we receive.

The quaint and sometimes misleading moniker "Christian hospitality" beckons mystery, births community, and bequeaths truth telling. Hospitality commands the kind of truth telling that makes your teeth stand on edge. It sounds domestic, but it really shakes the gates of heaven for the souls of the people you feed, hold, and love. The list making and grocery shopping make me small, meager, messy. It ties me to home and hearth and budget keeping. This busy preparation for the table fellowship that comes daily, and where Jesus lays his head, requires 50 percent prayer, 40 percent organization, and 10 percent hutzpah. Kent and I and our children shore up the 50 percent prayer; I put my hand on the plow of 40 percent organization; and interruptions, conflict, and unpredictability create 10 percent backdrop of every day, every list, every kiss on a child's cheek, every rebuke from the world or from the Lord, every setback, every lonely, cold finger of doubt. Faith in Jesus foregrounds the trust that says, "I love my neighbor because she is mine, and not because she loves me back."

3

Our Post-Christian World

The Kindness of Hospitality

July 1997, Syracuse, New York

Going to dinner at the home of Christians was not high on my list of longed-for activities. As an out-lesbian feminist, a leader in LGBTQ rights, the recent coauthor of the first domestic partnership policy at Syracuse University, and a soon-to-be tenured radical, my heart's desire was not to become friends with the enemy. Christians seemed like a small-minded, uncharitable, immoral bunch. They ate meat, believed in corporal punishment, violated human and environmental rights at a fevered pitch, denied a woman's right to choose, and believed that the whole world should fall under the totalitarian obedience to the Bible, an ancient book fraught with racism, sexism, and homophobia. They believed in and manufactured superstitions about "sin," which I believed was, as Freud declared, simply a cultural phobia deeply held by dupes whose thinking was manipulated by a universal obsessional neurosis. (Thank Freud for that meaningful mouthful.) But, mostly, Christians just scared me to death.

47

Our worldviews—and the moral lens we used to make sense of things—were incommensurable. Unbridgeable.

But there I was in their driveway, parking my red Isuzu Amigo truck decorated with my NARAL (National Abortion Rights Action League) bumper sticker and lesbian Labrys decals. I sat there in my truck readying myself to knock on the front door. I was developing a strategy about how to keep the conversation off of my "sin" (always a fetish for Christians, in my experience) and on the subject of why Christians read the Bible as a literal text—a hermeneutic which I saw as, all-hands-down, sloppy, nonprogressive, and dumb. I was a postmodern reader-response critic, and I believed that all literary texts find meaning in the reader's interpretation. It annoyed me to no end when people read literary works "against" their literary genre—like reading a birthday party invitation under the rules of a sonnet, never arriving at the right place because you can't find the iambic pentameter. Christians assimilate the distinct genre of Bible texts into didactic verse-a-day commands. How anti-intellectual! The inherent goodness of self (as Rousseau taught), the priceless progress made by science after Darwin, the advantageous understanding of personhood developed by psychology after Freud, and the equitable socialist culture of economic fairness after Marx all proved to me beyond a shadow of a doubt that human autonomy—leaving consenting adults alone to do what they feel is best—is central to human flourishing and a healthy, happy world.

Why Christians would not leave consenting adults alone to flourish and be joyful was beyond me.

So I sat in my truck in the driveway of this Christian home, musing about the book I was writing on the Religious Right and their policies, practices, and narratives of hatred against people like me. To do this, I knew that I had to read the Bible. And I also knew that I needed to somehow get inside the head of a true believer. I believed that only a wacko or an idiot would believe that an ancient book was more relevant and real than the kindness, charity, good practices, open-mindedness, and personal experience reflected in my lesbian community.

But I was also a serious scholar, an English professor by training and practice, and I told my students that they earn the right to critique only by reading the enemy's books. If you haven't read it, you have no right to interpret it. I did not have reading knowledge of Greek and Hebrew—the Bible's original languages—so I knew that I would need to find someone who did. I wanted to leave no stone unturned. I wanted to attack the Bible on legitimate and not straw-men's terms. I believed that scholars must be risk takers. We must take the risk of being wrong, and we must take the risk of reading things that offend. It is necessary to be this kind of scholar of integrity in order to confront the opposition with respect. So there I was, about to start writing a new book, but first I had to take on the book that condemned me, called me an abomination, castigated me, and assigned me to an eternity in hell.

And how in God's green earth did I get here, parked in the driveway of the enemy, you might ask?

The nice Christians who invited me to dinner intrigued me. The pastor—Ken Smith—wrote to me regarding an op-ed I had published in the *Syracuse Post Standard*.[1] In it, I opposed the Christian men's movement, Promise Keepers, for their backward and misogynist gender politics and their threat against democracy. I have always read all of my hate mail—call me a masochist—and I came to the conclusion that Ken's letter of opposition was the kindest one I had ever received. I also liked the fact that Ken had the right pedigree to help me with my research. When Ken and his wife, Floy, invited me to dinner, I said yes. My motives were clear: surely this would be good for my research. I considered Ken Smith my potential unpaid research assistant.

But the task at hand was daunting, and that is why I sat in my truck so long, not quite ready to knock on the front door of this house and walk across its threshold. Somehow, I would have to emerge from this meal understanding the oppressive logic that elevated a dead book above the desires of good people, and I would have to do so without having an emotional breakdown. To be hated for who you are carries insidious violence, and I had been on the receiving end of that before with Christians. Dealing with Christians was toxic work. Like deep-sea diving, you could stay down there only for so long before the long-term consequences took hold. I wanted to learn why Christians hated me so but maintain with integrity my point of view. The prospect made me sick to my stomach.

I breathed hard and hoisted myself out of my truck, nursing a tender hamstring from my morning run. I waded through the unusually thick July humidity to the front door, and I knocked.

The threshold to their life was like none other.

The threshold to their life brought me to the foot of the cross.

Nothing about that night unfolded according to my confident script. Nothing happened in the way I expected. Not that night, or the years after, or the hundreds of meals, or the long nights of psalm singing and prayer as other believers from the church and university walked through the door of this house as if no door was there. Nothing prepared me for this openness and truth. Nothing prepared me for the unstoppable gospel and for the love of Jesus, made manifest by the daily practices of hospitality undertaken in this one simple Christian home. This Christian home became my two-year refuge and way station. Long before I ever walked through the doors of the church, the Smith home was the place where I wrestled with the Bible, with the reality that Jesus is who he says he is, and eventually came face-to-face with him on the glittering knife's edge of my choice sexual sin. This Christian home was where I wrestled with my sexual identity and where I first dared ask the question, Is being a lesbian who I really am, or is it how the fall of Adam made me? Is it my authentic identity or the distorted one that came through the power of Adam's imputed and original sin to render my deep and primal feelings untrustworthy and untrue?

When I first stepped into the home of Ken and Floy Smith, I believed that religious liberty was a ruse that Christians used to garner unearned cultural capital. If you had told me twenty years ago that religious liberty is a manifestation of kindness, I would have laughed in your face. But that is what I now deeply and truly believe. Why? Why do Christians believe that religious liberty is a form of kindness, and how can we reflect this to our unbelieving neighbors? Have the moral changes in our society reflected God's kindness or something else?

Recently, Christian writer and blogger Tim Challies wrote about the three marks of a moral revolution, as reported in Theo Hobson's book *Reinventing Liberal Christianity*:[2]

1. What was universally condemned is now celebrated.
2. What was universally celebrated is now condemned.
3. Those who refuse to celebrate are condemned.

Tim leaves us with a question. He says, "Decide for yourself if this is, indeed, a moral revolution."[3] Decide for yourself if the world in which we live is post-Christian, if it has moved beyond the guidance of God, or worse, slandered God by claiming that his Word is not true.

The year 2015 was a decisive mark, representing a turning of the tide in the United States. *Obergefell v. Hodges*, the 2015 Supreme Court decision that legalized gay marriage and introduced the idea that sexual orientation determines who a person truly and deeply is, was truly a landmark decision. Whether you supported it or not, this court case left the world a different place than it was before.

For some, the *Obergefell* decision righted social wrongs and thereby made this world a better place. "Love wins" and "Love makes a family" became the slogans that stood behind what proponents called "marriage equality."

Since *Obergefell*, the gospel has been on a collision course with the idea that gay is who you are and not perhaps *how* you are. This idea, that who you are is better found in your sexual desires than in your image bearing of a holy God, has been brewing under the surface since the nineteenth century when Freud first introduced the cultural idea of sexual orientation.[4] This conflict has now exploded into the world.

Marriage equality rests on the idea that sexual orientation makes a person who she inherently or essentially is, that gay or lesbian describes who you are. Sexual identity, say proponents of marriage equality, determines personhood, and it must be protected by civil rights policy. But is this true? Is personhood determined by sexual desires (Freud's position) or by being made in God's image, male or female, with inherent ethical and moral responsibilities, constraints, and blessings (Gen. 1:27)?

Biblical marriage rests on the idea that marriage is created by God's design, but not everyone is designed for marriage. It rests on the idea that marriage is a creation ordinance by God's design, and that it cannot be changed even when the state tries to do that. It came before all we see and touch. And it shines the way forward, not only in the growing of families but, more vitally, in the mystery of the marriage between Christ and the church to which it points.

Are we at a stalemate? Is there no talking across our differences anymore? How did Ken and Floy and I become friends, real friends, anyway? If you believe, as I do, that religious liberty reflects biblical kindness, then consider the following practices.

1. Respect the Reality of Your Neighbors' Lives and Households

Ken and Floy Smith treaded carefully with me. Early in our friendship, Ken made the distinction between acceptance and approval. He said that he accepted me just as I was but that he did not approve. That seemed fair. But would it seem fair today?

Last year, an old friend came out to me as a lesbian. She called and said, "I've been avoiding telling you this, but I like girls. I know that you don't approve."

I was grateful that she called me. She is an old, dear friend, and I love her. So I asked her a simple question: "Do you think I wouldn't understand?"

She: "No, I know you understand. It's that you don't approve. I can't take knowing that you don't approve of me."

Me: "Did we always approve of each other?"

She: "No. No, we didn't."

Me: "We've disagreed on everything! Pixar films, chicken nuggets, spankings! We have never approved of each other, but we have always loved each other. True?"

She: "Very true. We've never approved. We've always loved."

Me: "So why are you changing the rules on me?"

My friend and I laughed and cried and argued—just like we had done for the ten years that we lived in the same community. But both geographic distance and worldview allegiance separate us. We are friends but not like we used to be. But we both are committed to this friendship—and to preserving its long history. It was important, though, to resist the idea that love and approval go hand in hand. Parents who love their children decidedly do not approve of everything they do. Part of being responsible brothers and sisters in Christ means knowing you can't give a good answer to a bad question.

Indeed, the issue that divides us must be confronted. Is acceptance the same thing as approval? When Ken Smith first told me twenty years ago that he accepted me but did not approve, I was not offended. The culture in which we all lived did not collapse the two. But today is a different story, and it is important to understand that. Today, to refuse to both accept and approve of those who identify as LGBTQ (etc.) is to deny their rights to determine for themselves what personhood means. This brings us to the epicenter of the worldview divide: whose image do we bear—the image of God, or the reflection of our sexual autonomy?

Unbelievers need to see genuine acceptance from us. They need to see genuine love. They need to see that being made in the image of God is a higher calling, bestowing a greater dignity, than inventing your own rules for faith and life.

With my unbelieving friends, I tread carefully. For example, I respect the rules of the LGBTQ community. I know these rules well. I helped make them. I remember the right names so that I don't confuse the children raised in LGBT homes. I know who is Mama and who is Mommy and I teach my children to get it right too. I speak to my neighbors with respect: "Are you wives to each other or partners?" I ask these questions because I care. I ponder: *Have I made myself safe to* share the real hardships of your day-to-day living, or am I still so burdened by the hidden privileges of Christian acceptability that I can't even see the daggers in my hands? Am I safe? If not, then why not? Even in a post-Christian world, we can claim unearned privileges rooted in sentimentality for days gone by. We can yearn for the 1950s in America or a medieval monastery. But sentimentality will lead only to discontent. Best stay right where we are, with eyes of faith open wide.

2. Pray That You Will Be a Safe Person to Hear the Burdens of Your Neighbors' Hearts

When the tears spill as a neighbor I love confesses that her partner finds her ugly and makes fun of her, I can gently move in, with warm hands, steaming mugs of strong coffee, and full eye contact, saying only this: *Jesus would never treat you like this. Jesus loves his daughters perfectly.* Do I have the grace to say this little? Or do I always have to say everything there is to say on a subject? If so, I am a brute and a boar. By grace, I put a guard over my mouth. I pray. Ephesians 4:29 shows me how: "Let no corrupting talk come out of your mouths, but only such as is good for building up, as fits the occasion, that it may give grace to those who hear." May my words give grace to those who hear. My words are not pep talks. I hope, indeed, that *my* words are not even my own but Christ's working through me. Invest in your neighbors for the long haul, the hundreds of conversations that make up a neighborhood, and stop thinking of conversations with neighbors as sneaky evangelistic raids into their sinful lives. Maybe our own lives are actually more sinful. Is it not more sinful to openly sin while claiming Christ's lordship than to sin while claiming false rights to self-autonomy? Stop treating your neighbor as a caricature of an alien worldview.

3. Understand the Biblical Difference between Holiness and Goodness and Don't Be Afraid to Celebrate the Goodness of Your Unbelieving Neighbors

It is a simple question: If my neighbors who identify as lesbian are in sin, then why are they the nicest people on the block? If our

Christian worldview cannot account for that, it can survive only in the echo chamber of imaginary theology.

God has bestowed much common grace on our neighbors—all of them—and we should be mighty thankful to God for this. Common grace is that kindness by God given to all of humanity—to the whole human race without distinction. Common grace curbs the destructive power of sin and can be found in God's providential care of creation (Heb. 1:2–3); his providential restraint of sin (Rom. 13:1); his work in the conscience of all people, helping and guiding all of us to see ourselves in eternal ways (Rom. 2:14–15); and his providential blessings in allowing friendships to form across deep divisions in worldview.

Because of the reality of God's common grace, we can say that our neighbors display goodness. We can love them and draw near to them. We can appreciate them and trust them.

But God's common grace is not enough to render any of us holy in his eyes. Common grace restrains sin on earth, but it does not remove the stain of sin from the giver's ledger. It's fruit, but it is not the good fruit that reflects a healthy vine. It gives from its plenty, not from its cross. It pays no ransom. Christian fruit hearkens from the cross it bears.

Someone may do very good things, things brimming with common grace, but if he has not repented and turned, placing all confidence in Christ for salvation, he will still—tragically—find eternity in hell. Common grace does not ingratiate us to God. Christ must rescue us; Christ must bleed for us; the Holy Spirit must comfort us. We must respond. Common grace is a works-driven blessing, and the Bible records our good works as filthy rags.

John Calvin's *Institutes of the Christian Religion* spells this out for us. Special grace is bestowed on those whom God has set apart. But how will you know who these people are—who we are—if you don't get close enough to have deep and abiding and personal and even awkward conversations, conversations that last over a lifetime?

And this reveals the kindness of the Reformed faith, which

compassionately knows that you are unable to save yourself, that to be deceived by sin means you have been taken captive by an evil force to do its bidding. It kindly knows that you need a rescuer, and God through his unconditional election rescues his people. It kindly reflects Jesus's substitutionary atonement—the Son of God takes on the ledger of our guilt and pays for it with his righteousness, becoming sin on our behalf, allowing us to become righteous on his merits. This call from God is irresistible grace—no matter how bad off we are, we are never hidden from God. And, finally, this kindness reveals itself in God's persevering with us.

And who, you might ask, is God's elect? Anyone with a broken spirit and a contrite heart. The Bible records this for us: "The sacrifices of God are a broken spirit; a broken and contrite heart, O God, you will not despise" (Ps. 51:17). If you worry about who you are before the Lord, pray that he will give you a broken and contrite spirit. Christ calls sinners to saving faith. The gospel call is for you and me and every person in the world.

God wants all to be saved: "Have I any pleasure in the death of the wicked, declares the Lord GOD, and not rather that he should turn from his way and live?" (Ezek. 18:23). About this verse Calvin writes: "How does God wish all men to be saved? He does this today by the Spirit's convicting the world of sin, righteousness, and judgment by the gospel. . . . God makes clear to people their great misery, so that they may come to him. He wounds so he may cure."[5] He wounds so he may cure. All affliction is meant to direct us to the fountain of life, Jesus Christ himself.

But this idea—that being convicted of your sin is a kindness of God—is antithetical to the idea that self-esteem is self-created. For your unbelieving neighbors to know the truth of God's love, you must manifest this broken and contrite heart. You must be close enough to be seen in transparent and vulnerable ways.

4. Don't Accuse of Ill Will People Who Hold to a Different Theology
Since LGBTQ became designators of personhood, of *who* rather than *how* a person is, we have seen many people depart from an

orthodox view of Scripture in favor of a progressive one. I do not believe that all these people have sold out. I believe that many of them are sick and tired of seeing their friends and family members who identify as LGBTQ made into straw men or women or reduced to political enemies to caricature on Facebook or in conversations after the sermon (or, even more horrifically, in the sermon). They wish to be an ally. They desire to stand in the gap for their friends. They want their friends to have the same rights and privileges as they do. They don't want to be a bigot—or even associate with bigots.

But those who depart from orthodoxy are unintentionally causing harm rather than good to those they love. The Bible, a unified biblical revelation, is our lifeline. This is important. Little-o orthodox Christians and liberal red-letter Christians are not standing in the same forest looking at different sides of the trees.[6] We are in different forests altogether. And that is a big problem. Do you believe that the gospel has the power to save? Do you believe that salvation comes without dying to self, all of self, all of you? The male/female binary, upon which biblical marriage rests, is essential to personhood and foundational to the creation mandate and to the gospel.

In a recent article at *Religion News Service*, David Gushee, who left evangelical Christianity in 2014, wrote:

> I now believe that incommensurable differences in understanding the very meaning of the Gospel of Jesus Christ, the interpretation of the Bible, and the sources and methods of moral discernment, separate many of us from our former brethren. . . . I also believe that attempting to keep the dialogue going is mainly fruitless. The differences are unbridgeable.[7]

I agree with Gushee that our differences are incommensurable and that our core difference is how we read the Bible. But I would never say that our differences are unbridgeable. That is a hopeless and heartless statement. Indeed, no one who believes that Jesus has risen from the grave could say that our differences are unbridgeable. The atoning blood of Christ is the bridge. There is a difference between theme Christianity (like the kind that Gushee articulates) and the real deal. Jesus lives, and that makes all the difference in the world. He bridges the unbridgeable. That is the point.

My red-letter friends want to be good neighbors toward people who think differently than I do, and I agree. And one important way that we can be good neighbors is to help people carry the crosses they bear. God's distribution of crosses is not democratic. I may get one cross, and you may get ten. The job of an ally is to accompany someone in her suffering and to carry some of the load of cross bearing. The job of an ally makes the cross lighter, not by erecting or supporting laws that oppose God's law, but by being good company in the bearing of its weight. By accompanying your friend in suffering. By standing close and staying near. By answering the phone at midnight, or, better yet, inviting her to move into your home while she wrestles with sin, the flesh, and the Devil. We are not extending grace to people when we encourage them to sin against God. Grace always leads to Christ's atoning blood. Grace leads to repentance and obedience. Grace fulfills the law of God, in both heart and conduct. When we try to be more merciful than God, we put a millstone around the neck of the person we wish to help.

5. Know Why It Matters Most That We Are Made in God's Image

If we are all children of the same God—made in his image—aren't we fine just as we are? What does it mean to have our identity in bearing the image of God?

The Westminster Shorter Catechism asks: *How did God create man?* The answer provided is this: "God created man male and female, after his own image, in knowledge, righteousness, and holiness, with dominion over the creatures." How are we made in God's image? Genesis 1:27 explains:

> So God created man in his own image,
> in the image of God he created him;
> male and female he created them.

God's creative power made male and female distinctive and valuable. The value of human life, to God, is inherent (who we are—image bearers), not instrumental (what we are able to do and accomplish). We are worthy because of our ontology—our origins—in God's image. Murder is the most evil of all sins because it destroys an image of God.

God also gives men and women distinct roles and tasks based on their sexual differences. God cannot sin, so these differences in gender roles are not arbitrary or offensive or dangerous. Being born male or female carries different blessings, constraints, and moral responsibilities. Sexual difference, and the gender identity that emerges from it, is a calling that God determines in his creation ordinance. It is not an arbitrary reflection of culture. It is hard to live up to this calling. God knows that, and that is why he gave us the Bible and his church and the family of God to help. Through those means we "put on the new self, which is being renewed in knowledge after the image of its creator" (Col. 3:10).

Christians are new creatures and are now identified by their union with Christ. Union with Christ is the greatest blessing that Christians have, and it sets us apart from those who do not know Christ. We have union with Christ in three interdependent ways. First is *immanent union*, which is having union with Christ from all eternity, and finally, at conversion, stepping into the true identity that God has been holding safe for us. Ephesians 1:4 explains this well. Second is *transient union*, which is having union with Christ in his death and resurrection and our identity born of this (Rom. 6:3–7). The third kind of union is *applicatory union*, the lived application of how Christ indwells and the Holy Spirit comforts and directs us today and forevermore (Eph. 2:5–7).[8]

Sanctification is a work, not an act. We grow in sanctification over a lifetime of living in union with Christ, of denying ourselves, of taking up the cross, of following Christ. We grow in knowledge of God when we read our Bible in the way God intends—as an inerrant, inspired, authoritative, unified revelation. Image-bearing the knowledge of God means that we lean into the cross and not into ourselves. There is always a battle between cross carrying and doing what feels best to us. But the Christian is a new man or woman. God calls us to conform our lives to Christ. This is excruciating. Growing in sanctification means that there is a growing tension between your union with Christ and your sexual identity.

How are we made in God's righteousness? Ephesians 4:24 explains: "Put on the new self, created after the likeness of God in true righteousness and holiness." There we see again the biblical contrast of putting on the new man and putting off the old man. This refers not only to specific sin patterns that may characterize a person's particular life but also to putting off our identity in Adam (whose imputed sin makes us guilty and corrupt before God) and putting on our identity in Christ (whose bloody love gives us the power we need to defeat the sin patterns that still seduce). We bear the image of God in righteousness when we renew our mind through the truth found in God's Word. If we deny that God's Word is fully true, even the hard parts, we tarnish God's image in ourselves.

How are we to steward the earth? Genesis 1:28 explains:

> And God blessed them. And God said to them, "Be fruitful and multiply and fill the earth and subdue it, and have dominion over the fish of the sea and over the birds of the heavens and over every living thing that moves on the earth."

Being created in the image of God has consequences and expectations. We find there a mandate to steward well—to care for, nurture, teach, and protect—the family and the world.

So, what is so "post-Christian" about our world? It's the idea that being a human being means both more and less than being an image bearer of a holy God. The real issue at the core is personhood. Failing to discern rightly who we are renders us unable to accurately discern anything we touch, feel, think, or dream. Failing to discern rightly who we are renders us unable to properly know who God is. We are truly lost in a darkness of our own making. And we are not innocent. As John records, the world's love of darkness is itself a manifestation of God's judgment, not our higher mindedness: "This is the judgment: the light has come into the world, and people loved the darkness rather than the light because their works were evil" (John 3:19).

Are Christians victims of this post-Christian world? No. Sadly, Christians are coconspirators. We embrace modernism's perks when they serve our own lusts and selfish ambitions. We despise modernism when it crosses lines of our precious moralism. Our cold and hard hearts; our failure to love the stranger; our selfishness with our money, our time, and our home; and our privileged back turned against widows, orphans, prisoners, and refugees mean we are guilty in the face of God of withholding love and Christian witness.

And even more serious is our failure to read our Bibles well enough to see that the creation ordinance and the moral law, found first in the Old Testament, is as binding to the Christian as any red letter. Our own conduct condemns our witness to this world. Shame on us. Our post-Christian world has not taken away our Bibles or the Holy Spirit's convicting rebuke on our Christ-owned consciousness. We have done this through high-minded moralism and unrepentant sin. And now we must be salt and light in a world that knows we have blown it. We will wear the title of hypocrite—and rightly so—until we repent to God and love our neighbor in word and deed. Now is the time to know our stuff and roll up our sleeves. Reconciliation starts with repentance.

In Christ we have all the rights and privileges of God's image bearers: noble birth, eternal life, and, through Christ, defeat of the stain of death and sin. We have adoption into the family of God and the privilege of a new nature, one that has the power that raised Christ from the dead in the form of the Holy Spirit working in us and through us, driving out the old man or woman and beckoning in the new. The Bible tells us who we are: essentially male or female, and the binaries that separate the two are divine and sacred and eternal. We are ontologically image bearers of God, with a need to have our heavenly Father's love. The gospel is good news for everyone, even those who have much to lose.

Henri Nouwen, the late and gentle Catholic priest and founder of the L'Arche Daybreak Community (for people with mental disabilities) in Toronto, Canada, regarded hospitality as a spiritual movement, one that is possible only when loneliness finds its spiritual refreshment in solitude, when hostility resolves itself in hospitality, and when illusion is manifested in prayer.

Because of the blood of Christ, because Jesus dined with sinners but did not sin with sinners, because repentance is the threshold to God, table fellowship is both comforting and challenging. It meets you where you are and asks you to die so that you can live.

Practicing hospitality in our post-Christian world means that you develop thick skin. The hospitable meet people as strangers and invite them to become neighbors, and, by God's grace, many will go on to become part of the family of God. This transition from stranger to neighbor to family does not happen naturally but only with intent and grit and sacrifice and God's blessing.

6. Start Somewhere. Start Today

One logical place to start is at the end of your driveway.

Our neighborhood (made up of three hundred houses in the city of Durham, North Carolina) uses a social media app called Nextdoor. This is the only form of social media in which I participate. If I am going to post a picture of my lunch, I want to be able to share it with those with whom I might actually share this lunch—my neighbors. I read Nextdoor updates daily, and I receive messages as they are posted so that I can respond to and pray for the neighbors whom I do not yet know. I pray about lost dogs, and I donate school supplies. Every time someone posts a request for meals for a sick, grieving, or newly blessed-by-newborn neighbor, I'm on it. I look carefully at the food allergies and preferences. Over the years, I have developed go-to recipes for a variety of food needs. If the meal goes to a new mom, I include my favorite mom book, Gloria Furman's *Missional Motherhood*.[9] (And yes, I have read other books on motherhood—most of them, really, as I am some-what obsessed with reading about motherhood, and this one is the very best.)

While others brag about how cheap they are when it comes to hospitality, Kent and I budget for it, and it hurts. Practicing daily, ordinary, Christian hospitality doubles our grocery budget—and sometimes triples it. There are vacations we do not take, house projects that never get started, entertainment habits that never get an open door, new cars and gadgets that we don't even bother coveting. Our children will never be Olympic-level soccer stars, wear designer clothes, or have social calendars requiring a staff of drivers. Instead, my children build forts and catch frogs in the backyard, eat popsicles in trees, and bring neighborhood kids to dinner and devotions when the bell rings.

It costs money and time and heartache to run a house that values radically ordinary hospitality and nightly table fellowship, and we are all in. Over the past sixteen years of marriage, we have given away a lot of things. We give away many meals each week (those we serve here, those we serve at church, those we send in Pyrex pans to neighbors who have new babies or new knees, and those we mail to brothers and sisters in prison via iCare packages). We give away our time. We share our house. We don't rent space in our house. If we did that, we wouldn't be able to give it away. We give away cars when we have had the means to do so. We have never suffered for the absence of anything.

Paul's words ring in my ears: "To me, though I am the very least of all the saints, this grace was given, to preach to the Gentiles the unsearchable riches of Christ, and to bring to light for everyone what is the plan of the mystery hidden for ages in God, who created all things" (Eph. 3:8–9). I like better the King James rendering: "And to make all men see what is the *fellowship* of the mystery . . ."

Fellowship of the Mystery

Christian hospitality brings together the mystery of union with Christ and the fellowship of the saints to gather in close the stranger and the outcast and the chronically lonely. We make gospel bridges into our home because we notice the people around us and their needs. We see people whom God has put into our lives—especially the difficult ones—as image bearers of a Holy God and therefore deserving of our best. Hospitality is image-bearer driven, because Christ's blood pumps me whole. It is not time, convenience, and calendar driven. If it were, none of it would happen. None of this grace would be mine to hold and to share.

Hospitality requires daily Bible reading, deep repentance, dark mornings in solitude, and the daily willingness to forgive others whether or not they ask.

Hospitality renders our houses hospitals and incubators. When I was in a lesbian community, this is how we thought of our homes. I learned a lot in that community about how to shore up a distinctive culture within and to live as a despised but hospitable and compassionate outsider in a transparent and visible way. I learned how to create a *habitus* that reflected my values to a world that despised me.

I learned to face my fears and feed my enemies.

So here I am. A new creature in Christ, yes, but still wearing my Birkenstocks. Lobotomized, no. A beneficiary of God's grace, both common and saving, with eyes wide open to behold what contagious grace looks like—and what it does to people and the world and the church. And my house, by God's grace, is still an incubator and a hospital.

4

God Never Gets the Address Wrong

The Providence of Hospitality

Winter 1972, River Forest, Illinois

I was raised in an Italian community in River Forest, Illinois, by two excommunicated Catholics. I loved my parents, and they loved me, but love has only the integrity of the lover, as Toni Morrison once said, and raw, emotive love-as-ownership, fueled by too much alcohol and too many diet pills, never stays in its own lane. It's ruthless. It's brutal.

My mother was a relentlessly hard worker. She woke up before anyone else in the house and stayed up long into the night. My mother, trained as a medical technologist, owned a medical laboratory. After school every day, I went to my mom's lab to do my homework in her office. I was raised to know that my mom was smart, could run a business, and was very much in charge.

My dad was implacably handsome and would have been a playboy had other life experiences not cornered off this impulse. He had weathered job and school and marriage failures (both my parents had previous divorces), and eventually he became a labor leader for the Chicago Teamsters Union. My father was a charismatic public speaker. I remember going with him to union meetings, my father pumping his fists in the air like a prizefighter, commanding a large stage with hundreds of men in blue work pants and work-issue gray shirts cheering, smoking, cussing, and clapping. While I really didn't see the magic in my father's words, his intended audience was hanging on his every word. The greater the applause, the more my father lit up. He stood 5 feet 8 inches tall—which counts for tall in my family—and when he spoke to a crowd, he looked larger than life. He had shining black hair, slicked back 1950s style with Alberto VO5. His violet-blue eyes were piercing. My father had his nails done and hair trimmed at a salon every three weeks. I thought he resembled a Greek god.

My brother—my father's son from his first marriage—was eight years older than I. He shared heroin from our garage, shot up in the family bathroom, and fondled himself on the living room couch while watching afternoon TV. He was not a terribly bad guy, as I remember him.

My mother dutifully made sure that I had the best classically educated childhood possible. I attended predominantly Catholic schools—excellent ones, with diligent and disciplined nuns. I learned in Catholic school to love language and hard work. I loved the nuns and even thought about becoming one some day, not because of faith but because of community, of the peace I imagined would come from living in a service-motivated home with other women. I'm named after the rosary, and while I never knew to whom I prayed, the chanting peace of the rosary was my daily comfort.

My favorite childhood memories were of my parents hosting parties. Someone would start playing the piano and my mother would sing. Oh, how I loved to hear my mother sing! She had a powerful contralto voice and would belt out all the verses to all the show tunes—*Oklahoma*; *Hello, Dolly!* I have a cassette tape of her singing "My Romance," which was her audition song for musicals and commercials in New York when she was twenty-five.

My parents gave me the best of what they had, but lofty goals and good intentions were no match for the sin patterns that took my family by storm.

Once, my dad took me on an "errand." I was nine years old, and that was the last "errand" on which I was ever allowed to accompany him.

We parked the car. He was driving a pink Lincoln Continental at the time. (We called it the Pink Link.) I was in the front seat. (This was back in the old days when children were not restricted to car seats until reaching seventeen years of age or 5 feet 4 inches tall.) We drove into the cemetery by our house, the same cemetery that Dad would later use to teach me how to drive. He said that it was a safe place because a new driver couldn't kill anyone here—they were already dead. Dad drove deep into the cemetery and parked the Pink Link in a circle of gray stone graves and sloping trees. It was four o'clock and would soon be dark. The day was mild, and oaks swathed large shadows over my folded hands.

Dad told me to get down and stay on the floor and warned me to not show myself, no matter what. He locked me in the car. I tasted the sweat of fear.

I heard another car drive up, screeching the tires as it came to a halt. Loud male voices shouted vulgarities. My father had another side, an evil, angry, violent side. He kept that side hidden at home. He unleashed it here. I heard crashing and a sharp snapping that sounded like a whip. Then screaming—guttural and animal-like. And then the voices stopped, and I heard the other car screech into forward motion and peel out of the parking lot. My father started moaning. No one was there to hear him except a daughter saying the rosary on the car floor and the silent graves. I chanted as quickly as I could, trying to beat the clock to the stages of the cross. But the shadows faded, dark enveloped the car, my father's sobbing turned to weeping, and someone approached the car. It wasn't God.

It was my father. I heard him crying out in pain, and I was too ashamed to do anything but silently chant, "Hail Mary, full of grace, the Lord is with thee . . . "

When he crawled to the car, his feet were a bloody mess. The shoes he was wearing had been carved into the pavement because, when the other car peeled off, my father had been hanging on to the open window.

He was shaking as he unlocked the car and collapsed in the front seat.

He smelled of sweat and fear and blood and urine and cigarettes.

His body gyrated with convulsive shaking, and he gripped the wheel and drove us home. His teeth spasmed and convulsed.

I looked away, trying to give him privacy, trying to give him anything that could come close to dignity.

He drove home with feet that had layers of skin peeled off by raging pavement.

I needed a God who was going to come and get me, because I could not find him on my own. I needed a God who could come get me on the floor of my father's car. I was buried in layers of terror, rings of family violence, and the shame of my own churning and rage. The good was inseparable from the evil, the love indistinguishable from the manipulation. I craved the former without the latter, but these were package deals in my childhood. I needed a gospel that went as deep as the terror that hunted me down and haunted me. Did such a God exist? Is there really a God who lives in this world?

Did I have Christian neighbors, I wonder now? Neighbors who knew? Neighbors who could have helped my family?

June 1974, Fort Lauderdale, Florida

Carlos was my favorite older cousin. Growing up, he was my babysitter on Saturday nights when my parents would go out to parties and stumble home drunk. Carlos would pop big bowls of popcorn and slather them in butter and salt, and then we'd both get out our knitting and crocheting. He'd turn the TV to our favorite program, *Creature Features*. We would knit and talk and laugh. He was always kind and gentle. He let me eat popcorn for dinner and stay up as late as I wanted. He never made fun of me or did things that scared me, as my brother did. We both liked reading Jane Austen novels. Carlos was fifteen years older than I.

When he was twenty-five, Carlos came out to the family as gay. Soon after, he started posing for *Playgirl* magazine (my parents kept a subscription to both *Playboy* and *Playgirl* in the bathroom. I suppose they believed in equal-opportunity porn). Carlos was the first owner of the Cathode Ray gay bar in Fort Lauderdale, Florida. (In some circles, the Cathode Ray is infamous.) I, my parents, aunts, uncles, cousins, and Grandma were all at the bar's opening night.

Carlos was restless on that opening night. He bathed meticulously, fussed with his tuxedo, applied too much Mont Blanc, and merely toyed with the scrambled eggs I cooked for him.

When we entered through the doors of the Cathode Ray, I knew I had never seen a place like it. I was twelve years old, and that was the first time, but not the last, that I would spend a Sunday night in a gay bar. The bar had different sections. On the dance floor were men dancing with men and women dancing with women. My whole body tingled in a way I could not control when I saw that. The image of a woman's embrace drew my breath away. The sensation felt wrong, in a way that drew me like a riptide in an open sea. At the bar was the older crowd, my parents drinking and showing off, and men—mostly men—toasting and laughing and smoking. It was very loud. And then off in a corner I saw two men in white underwear and nothing else. That seemed so funny to me! It wasn't that hot outside. I had no idea why anyone would go out in public in white underwear! I found a chair with my younger cousins; we drank ginger ale and played hangman on the bar's napkins.

My cousins and I were used to going to bars with our parents and to casinos in Las Vegas. We thought this was normal. So we played hangman and tic-tac-toe. We thought this club would be like the casinos in Vegas. But as the night went on, I saw people do things that I did not think people did. This was different from any other bar to which my parents took me. There was a seductive darkness. The bar filled with more and more people. After dark, the people came in wearing costumes. Some people came with props too. Was that cage with the men dancing a prop? And then I fell asleep.

That was the first, but it was not to be the last, gay bar I would frequent.

On June 12, 2016, Omar Mateen, a twenty-nine-year-old security guard, killed forty-nine people and wounded fifty-three others in a terrorist attack inside Pulse, a gay nightclub in Orlando, Florida. Immediately, media started to represent Pulse as a sanctuary rather than as a nightclub. Christians who, by God's grace and protection, had never stepped through the door of a gay club, concurred. A nightclub is a sanctuary, they said. Wesley Hill, in an article entitled "If the Church Were a Haven," a *First Things* article, offered this: "Clubs like Pulse have been among the precious few places for the LGBTQ community throughout its history to find respite from ridicule (and worse). . . . Some of the clubs have even borne that name—'Sanctuary'—in neon, like a lighthouse pointing the way to safety."[1]

It is a misleading article, and it is based on a shamefully misleading idea. Gay clubs, some of which are explicitly sex clubs, are examples of dangerous and dark sins, all falling under the category of counterfeit hospitality. They capitalize on a deep longing, a powerful desire, a genuine need to belong. And they sell you a counterfeit comfort—and worse. And "sanctuary" is the antithesis of what it is. After work and until about ten thirty, gay clubs can be places where people gather to discuss politics and health care, to meet up with friends for happy hour, to celebrate after a bowling tournament. But after a certain hour they become dark places. God knows. Galatians records:

> Now the works of the flesh are evident: sexual immorality, impurity, sensuality, idolatry, sorcery, enmity, strife, jealousy, fits of anger, rivalries, dissensions, divisions, envy, drunkenness,

orgies, and things like these. I warn you, as I warned you before, that those who do such things will not inherit the kingdom of God. (Gal. 5:19–21)

The stark truth of that verse does not condone bigotry.

It does not condone gay jokes, which are never funny.

It does not condone talking about people instead of listening to them.

Our lack of genuine hospitality to our neighbors—all of them, including neighbors in the LGBTQ community—explains why counterfeit hospitality seems attractive. Our lack of Christian hospitality is a violent form of neglect for their souls.

But the terrorist attack at Pulse does not condone naive and misguided Christians misappropriating personal experience. Christians too often fear offending people for not using their words. But we can also offend people by using their words in a way that yanks them from their context. Words make worlds, and the only word that can navigate truth is the Word made flesh, Jesus, the rescuer of people like me. When we change the language, we change the logic.

A nightclub is not a sanctuary. No one really believes that it is.

Going Back to School

We flew back to Chicago the following day.

My memories of the Cathode Ray grew hazy. I could still capture images and smells. These images both shocked and seduced me. I longed to recapture them, and I shuddered at the possibility. When I saw from the corner of my eye the men in the cage, my brain went numb. Did I really see that? I couldn't have really seen that, right?

The next day I woke up early and put on a crisp, white blouse and a clean, navy-blue plaid skirt. I did what I always did: I compartmentalized. My night at the Cathode Ray was a different life from my life as a Catholic schoolgirl. We flew out of Fort Lauderdale while the sky was still morning dark. Dad drove me to school directly from the airport, just in time to make the afternoon bell. As he hugged me and kissed me goodbye, he said the same thing that he said every day when he parked the car in the school parking lot: "Be good, be polite, learn a lot, and don't believe anything the nuns tell you." My parents felt religion stifled the imagination. (With flashbacks from the Cathode Ray, I would have welcomed a decrease in imagination, at least on that morning.)

I hopped out of the car and greeted my favorite nun, Sister Mary Margaret, at the door. I recited my Latin declensions and drafted my Emily Brontë paper in my two favorite classes, Latin and English. I worked on my knitting during break. I sat with Irene at prayer time. I memorized my lines from *Joseph and the Amazing Technicolor Dreamcoat*. I tried to pretend I was normal. Sometimes pictures from the club flashed into my brain like a light switch, calling my affections to a dark place. I knew two things about that place: it was dark, and it was drawing me. At catechism that afternoon, Father Paul was talking about how the resurrection was a metaphor. My Catholic life was in a compartment too. A metaphor works on the power of the page. A metaphor is not real or alive or any of that. A metaphor cannot be true. Perhaps if the resurrection was a metaphor, it explained why Jesus could not follow me to the Cathode Ray or to my parents' home or to any other place where I really needed him.

I thought a lot about sin that day, especially original sin. Sister Mary Margaret taught me that original sin was like being born with a big bleach spot on my navy-blue skirt. I looked at my skirt, and I didn't really think it would be too terribly ugly with a bleach spot. I fingered the stiff fabric and tried to imagine how big of a bleach stain my original sin would make. Original sin didn't sound ugly. Maybe it would look sort of tie-dyed. Original sin, she said, meant that we are born without grace. Each time I went to Mass, each time I took the host in my mouth and drank the wine, God would fill in that bleach spot with more grace, until one day I would be all whole, and my blue skirt would not have an ugly bleach stain. The Virgin Mary's blue skirt was all filled in before she became baby Jesus's mother. That's why we pray, "Hail Mary, full of grace." Her original sin was taken away so that she could be the mother of Jesus. If only I could be full of grace, maybe bad things would not happen to me. I set my mind to working harder and trying to get to Mass as often as I could.

I was banking on salvation by sacrament.

Life Goes On

I rarely brought friends home. Home was unpredictable at best. I didn't mind the alone time, though, and I had my cousins who lived on the same block. I was in middle school; my brother had moved out permanently; my parents fought less but drank more; and I spent my after-school time in my room with my homework, my cats, and my knitting. When someone from school invited me to her home for dinner or a birthday party, I would go. I would marvel at how relaxed other people could be with their parents. I was always waiting for my parents to unleash mounting anger or to stumble around drunk and passionate. I was always embarrassed to be me. And I was always accumulating ways to distract my parents from their anger or their passions. I learned early on to make up ludicrous stories about the cats. Both my parents loved cats and found my anthropomorphic tales about them amusing. I tried to reconcile what Sister Mary Margaret taught me about original sin with what I saw in my own heart and in my parents' home. But it did not seem to me that we had bleach stains on our skirts. It seemed to me that we had blood stains that infected every vein and capillary. A gospel of respectable morality for respectable people wasn't going to come close to the knife that pierced my heart. Who could open my heart, see what was inside, and make me new? If the resurrection was a metaphor, I had little confidence that Mass would make all things new.

Did I have Christian neighbors, neighbors who might have helped?

Who knew?

February 1998, Syracuse, New York

I was writing books, giving lectures, directing dissertations, and teaching undergraduate and graduate classes. I ran the under-graduate studies program in English and textual studies at Syracuse University. I was a rising star. I was out to change the world. I wasn't looking for more friends, and certainly not friends who thought I was a sinner.

To this day I really can't explain why Ken and Floy and I became such good friends, except for a few simple truths.

The first is that Ken and Floy wouldn't let go of me. I tried to disappear, which should not have been hard, given that we traveled in different circles of influence. But they were a ministry team, and they just wouldn't let go. Every week, one or the other would check in, either by phone or email. It became easier to join them for weekly meals than to dodge them. Don't get me wrong—the Smiths weren't pests or stalkers. But they were unshakably present. Only later did I understand that no one can dodge people who are *prayerfully* present. Ken and Floy prayed for me—their arch-enemy—every day. They thought about me, and they prayed for me like I was their daughter. That created a vortex of understanding, worked out in the heavenly realm, away from which I could not run.

The second common bond is that I was secretly smitten with Ken and Floy's hospitality. People of all stripes came and went. Floy's meals were like mine: simple and plentiful. We both served a lot of rice and beans. Floy's kitchen cabinets were lined with large mason jars filled with beans of many colors. At the end of a parade of colorful bean jars was one cookbook: *More with Less: Suggestions by Mennonites on How to Eat Better and Consume Less of the World's Limited Food Resources.*

People came into the Smith home with their Bibles (that was new) and Psalters (a collection of psalms set to four-part a cappella music and used like a song book, which was new and kind of cool, as all things ancient truly are to any genuine humanities scholar). The people who walked through Ken's door were both culturally and musically literate, and they knew how to open a book and read it. They also knew how to work out the tenor part of a psalm written in four-part harmony. I respected these skills. Reading music and ancient texts is a rare art, and I felt magnetized by their quiet and unassuming skills.

The people who gathered at the Smith house were deep, practiced, and thoughtful, even if I thought that they were dead wrong. They also read the Bible differently from any other book I have seen people open up in public settings. They read the Bible in the first-person present tense. They not only said that they believed it was a living book owned by God himself; they treated it like it was. In prayer, they talked to God as if they were on good terms with him.

But when they opened up the Psalter, something deep inside me came alive. Four-part harmony, without fail. Ron on bass, Diana on alto, any number of sincere homeschooled boys with popping pimples on tenor, sopranos who lightly graced the top of the music without bringing attention to themselves. I was reminded of a choir director in music school who talked about four-part harmony like a house: the basement foundation (bass), the floor (tenor), the walls (alto), the roof (soprano). The singing at the Smith house built a balanced house. So rare, I pondered. The quality of music was excellent, but the words they sang were startling, disarming, offensive, even vile. The music was like a hot, South American, black bean chili with a hint of honey. It lingered, and you couldn't tell if it was hot or sweet, until you bit into a live pepper and the tears flowed uncontrollably. The music of the Psalms called something out from me, something that ranged between bitter rage and secret consent.

The third common bond is that we both liked our enemies close, and that was clear by the open door of their home. This was a skill that I wanted to learn from them. In theory, I often said the same thing. I said things like, "Where everyone thinks the same, no one thinks very much." I said, "Keep your enemies close; like a kicking horse, they can't wind up to hit you hard when you stand close." But still, year after year, my table fellowship consisted mostly of the same white, lesbian-identifying PhDs in the humanities. Not diverse, in spite of all our intersectional claims on oppression. The only exception was the occasional adopted daughter from China. The AIDS crisis diversified our gender. And J, my transgender friend, diversified our gender identity. But for the most part, the core people were all alike.

Here I was—an enemy—writing a book against these people. And here I was, enjoying myself in spite of the vast worldview divide that was real and true and vital to all of us.

And this wasn't a one-time thing, like an occasional poem written on behalf of a truce in a war. This was a thing—a weekly thing for me, but, I suspected, a daily thing for them. This is how these Christians lived, and it was compelling and powerful. In spite of everything, Ken and Floy, Ron and Robyn, Dee, Bill, Renee, Nora, and Bud had become my pack. At least on Sunday nights, which they called the "Lord's Day."

I didn't show up every week. I couldn't bear it. But they did. Of that I was sure.

Time did unnatural things at the Smiths' house on Lord's Day evenings. No rushing, no paper grading, no frantic phone calls with colleagues gossiping about other colleagues. No strategy meetings. I learned to clean up my foul mouth, at least on Sunday nights.

I was the chair of the ETS program—English and textual studies. We boasted being the first English department in the country to abandon traditional English studies at the undergraduate level for a poststructural and cultural-theory-based curriculum. Gone was English composition 101. That plebeian grunt class was demoted to the writing program, a separate academic unit, even housed in a different building. Writing and composition, like old-school reading of classic literature according to its authorial specter, was out. Reader-response, pomo (postmodern), critical theory replaced it. We who ran this revolution even called ourselves (privately) the Pomo Homos. We considered it a compliment.

At the Smiths' house, Pastor Ken was leading what they called "family devotions," going through the book of James. I was fascinated. James was a terribly practical book, I thought, and fascinating in its simplicity.

James also had some zingers for me.

Gossip, the tongue on fire, curse words.

How would I talk with my colleagues if we were not gossiping about other colleagues?

How could I get through a sentence without a curse word?

But the best part of the evening was the singing.

People with musical literacy are hard to find, and I was thrilled to have found them. In my day-to-day world we had the gay male choir—and they were very, very good. But somehow lesbians of my circle were not into this. And so in my LGBTQ community, I was relegated to the audience. Singing the Psalms in four-part harmony was sensuous in a new way.

I even practiced at home, warming up my voice for our "Psalm sings."

Once as I was singing scales as a vocal warm-up for Psalm singing, my partner looked at me with a cocked eyebrow:

"What exactly do you *do* at the cult house?"

That's how we referred to Ken and Floy's house: "the cult house."

I despised them, I mocked them, I made sport of our Bible reading and Psalm singing, and they loved me, and included me, and prayed for me.

"Warming up my vocal cords," I answered. As if this is the most ho-hum thing for me to do.

I had tried meditation.

I had dutifully rolled out my yoga mat, lit my smudge of patchouli and lavender, and lowly hummed, "Ummmmm."

I joined meditation and reading groups, poring over the details in Thich Nhat Hanh and Shunryu Suzuki. But I couldn't generate any peace from the inside. Inside of me burbled up toil and trouble. It was as if Pandora belched every time my heart beat.

Truth be told, it hadn't really bothered me before now that discord multiplied out of my mouth. Postmodernism makes peace with discord. But the Bible valued the binaries I loathed. And the psalms were rooting deep inside me, as words do when you respect them enough to sing them.

These Christians talked about a peace that came from outside, from God himself.

That was new information.

If this Christian community that gathered weekly at the Smiths' house was a little bit like my LGBTQ community—especially in its home-based table gathering and its not-by-invitation-only flow— it was absolutely nothing at all like my family of origin. But this Christian community was also *more* than my LGBTQ community— and I saw that. This community was not left alone to their good intentions. God had found them out, and they were on good terms with him. How does such a thing happen, I wondered?

October 2015, Durham, North Carolina

"Why are we friends?" my awkward neighbor Hank asks as we are walking our dogs during a two o'clock, mid-afternoon home-school break, on a mild, fall North Carolina day, the blue sky shouting its glory for all to behold. Hank, a little light sensitive, twitches as his eyes adjust to the noon sun. He looks like he has just woken up.

"I mean, why don't you think I'm an eyesore and an oddball, like my neighbors in Chatham did?"

One of the many things I love about Hank: his bold questions, never holding back anything that others politely bury in social acceptance.

"Because God never gets the address wrong," I reply.

He looks at me from the side of his face as he adjusts the training collar around my dog. "You put this thing on backwards again. Here, let me get it on right," he offers, as we stop and put our dogs on a "sit stay" command. Hank nimbly drops to one knee to adjust my dog's training collar.

"I've never heard that before, about God not getting the address wrong," he sighs. "You really believe that?"

"I sure do."

"Is that another Christian thing?"

"It sure is."

Hank ponders that for a silent moment. Then he looks at the blue sky, pumps his arm upward, and exclaims, "Okay, kids, you lead the way! Tank and I need a good, long walk this afternoon! Where to? Meadow? Streets?"

Dismissing the painful subject of friendship, Hank shouts behind, as my children, fresh on a homeschool break, are also anxious to stop the babbling and get on with our hike.

"Oh, Mr. Hank, let's go trespassing again!" my children wail with joy, knowing that this will keep us far and long from the homeschool table.

Hank whoops. "These are my kind of kids!" he hollers, while the dogs pick up their steps. "Trespassing" is code for, "Let's walk through the big meadow in the open lot behind our houses." It is open property, but a big city builder has come in and wants to purchase it and build five hundred new units. Our neighborhood is fighting it. This property is needed as a buffer for the too-close highway as well as open meadow for wildlife. We love to walk through there while we all talk about what we love best about it. It is our favorite four-mile, mid-afternoon hike. It isn't trespassing yet, but it will be if the builder seals the deal.

When we pass other neighbors, I receive disquieted glares. A lot of people still haven't met Hank. So I stop and introduce Hank to every neighbor we pass. I say, "Mr. Moore, meet Hank. Hank and his mom bought Ellie's old house on the corner, the house with whom we share the open woods. Hank, this is Mr. Moore. He lives on the corner there, with the Knockout roses." Hands clasp, eyes soften, names exchange.

———

The first time Hank and I walked our dogs together was in August 2015. Kent and I had been trying to get to know this quiet, reclusive neighbor, but to no avail. Other neighbors had been gossiping about him. Kent consistently reminded those suspicious neighbors that words can tear people down and that Christians are not called to find fault just because someone is reclusive and quiet.

We had just taken in Sully, our tripod, goofball Gordon setter mixed with Thing 1 and Thing 2. We got him from the golden retriever rescue, but I won't tarnish the reputation of golden retrievers by implying that any member of this breed had anything to do with Sully. Nonetheless, we were successful at paying full price for a golden and coming home with a forty-pound black setter mutt with a missing left front leg. Sully was raw, undisciplined energy and enthusiasm. His leash walking was abysmal, his cat chasing superb, his garden digging extraordinary, and his nose could root out a rodent ten miles away. And even though he was born without his left front leg, he could dig holes in the backyard and run fast enough to catch a chipmunk in his soft mouth and plop it on the kitchen floor, the rodent shock-paralyzed but unharmed except for the untold emotional trauma. If God had ever said, "If your snout causes you to stumble, cut it off," he would have had Sully in mind. Sully hated his crate and had come to the golden retriever rescue from the high-kill dog pound. He was on his last day. (And, really now, how hard is it to find your three-legged dog in the pound? Usually there is only one at a time in residence.) At the golden retriever rescue, Sully wore out his welcome by eating a couch. Yes, you read that right. This dog ate a couch. At our house, he destroyed his metal crate on the first day, figuring out how to bend the metal bars as though he had super Houdini powers.

This was our kind of dog.

And Sully loved my son Knox, and my son loved this crazy dog.

On day one, the kids and I went outside with Sully on a leash and halter collar, attempting to take a walk.

As Sully was lunging me off my feet, Hank looked up from his yard work and said, "You need some help?" That was his first real sentence to me, excluding hellos and comments about the fine weather.

"Yes, please," I said.

And that is how we became friends, and how our household and Hank's became invested in one another.

He walked over to inspect the situation, getting down on the ground, compelling Sully to ease his tension on the leash and melt into Hank's lap. Sully softened into Hank's firm hand and tender voice. Hank was transformed by this disabled dog. "You are as rough around the edges as I am, Buddy," he said to no one in particular. Feeling the sinews and muscles that buffered a missing limb, Hank muttered almost to himself, "And broken, too."

Hank looked up at me, stroking my dog behind his ears, and asked, "Where did you get this one?" I explained Sully's history, and Hank offered to help me with dog training.

I had no idea if this man really could train a dog.

Not thinking he would take me up on it, I said, "Okay, let's start now. You walk my dog, and I'll walk yours."

He snatched a quick look at my eyes, sincerity checking, I assumed, and then quickly averted his glance and muttered, "Sure, let me run in and get a leash." Hank left me with my goofball dog jumping out of his skin and returned with Tank on a clothesline. Hank held up the clothesline and laughed, saying, "This will do for now. I'll go out later today and buy a leash. Tank will love this. Nobody ever asks me to walk dogs together."

Hank took my dog, and I took his, and so began a fragile friendship.

After we helped find Tank when he ran away for a week, our friendship was sealed. Our family became Hank's safe place.

And he became our friend who could fix anything, our friend who could find our goofy dog when he ran away to the next zip code, our friend who did not mock our faith but also did not see how in the world it applied to him.

Hank spent the first year of our friendship coming only into our front yard.

That's fine. We do a lot of hospitality in the front yard.

We have seen this before, the hesitancy of entering a home. Perhaps people fear being trapped in a place they can't easily leave. Perhaps people feel unwelcome, unable to grasp the strange landscape of perceived Christian mores and malarkey. How was it that when Jesus walked the earth, Jesus welcomed sinners and sinners welcomed Jesus? How did he get people to walk through the door? Take for example Luke 7:

> One of the Pharisees asked him to eat with him, and he [Jesus] went into the Pharisee's house and reclined at table. And behold, a woman of the city, who was a sinner, when she learned that he was reclining at table in the Pharisee's house, brought an alabaster flask of ointment, and standing behind him at his feet, weeping, she began to wet his feet with her tears and wiped them with the hair of her head and kissed his feet and anointed them with the ointment. Now when the Pharisee who had invited him saw this, he said to himself, "If this man were a prophet, he would have known who and what sort of woman this is who is touching him, for she is a sinner." (vv. 36–39)

This scene is disarming for many reasons, not the least of which is the total improbability of having an uninvited and unwelcome woman of ill repute crash a party and start fondling the guest of honor. It's preposterous. Someone would have stopped her at the door, no?

Well, yes and no.

If there had been a door, someone likely would have stopped her. But there was no door.

Well-to-do homes—like the one in this scene—had semi-public courtyards that were visible and open. Some gatherings were private and might have taken place in inner chambers. But most dinner parties resembled the Greco-Roman symposium, which literally means, "a convivial meeting . . . for drinking and intellectual conversation" or "a philosophical dialogue."[2] The space was large, with long tables of food and couches on which diners reclined. While all were not welcome at the table, "visitors could see what was happening and even contribute to what was being said. People could readily come in off the streets to pay their respects to the householder or to transact business. The poor, too, might hang around hoping for leftovers."[3]

My neighbors Ryan and Kristin have a house with a semi-public space. It is a large carport that faces the side of the house and is visible from two streets. They call it a party patio. I call it a carport with Christmas lights. They use this space as an enormous outdoor dining room. It has tables—small Little Tykes ones, patio tables, mismatched chairs, and one mighty cedar table that Ryan and Kristin spent a summer building together. (Kristin is a woodworker, and her house and yard reflect her amazing skill.) Ryan likes to say of this outdoor dining room, "We build tables, not walls, around here." There are no barriers to entering this space. And it is no palace. It is a large carport with good street visibility in the kind of busy North Carolina city/community where we lock our car doors at night and where we receive regular reports of home robberies. But Ryan and Kristin know how to build community. They thrive on it. They have the heart, and they have the touch.

I have watched how laughter and the smell of coffee and fajitas draw in other neighbors to this semi-public dining room. For Kristin's fortieth birthday party (in December), we gathered forty-strong, and Ryan rented propane-gas patio heaters and positioned them in the corners of the carport. The wind blew cold, the coffee poured warm, and we ate, drank, and bowed our heads in prayers of thanksgiving for this first-class daughter of the King whom the Lord had given to Ryan for his great blessing.

When Jesus walked the earth, the larger homes made use of such outdoor dining space. In Luke 7 the uninvited woman did not crash the party. The woman was likely a bystander drawn to the outdoor space much like neighbors pour in to the party patio at Ryan and Kristin's house. Jesus drew this woman despite her fear of rejection or gossip or threats or even potential violence from the homeowner. She brought what she knew to bring, which caused onlookers to take great offense.

She is described as "a woman of the city, who was a sinner" (v. 37). This is code for prostitute. She was a known prostitute. But Jesus did not seem to care about what the world knew her for. The scene unfolds an awkward moment. A known prostitute touches the known prophet in the only way she knows how to touch—with oil and loosened hair, which she uses to wipe the feet of her Lord. This was intimate—excessively so, given this woman's history with intimacy.

But Jesus does not rebuke her. When Jesus receives the repentance of a sinner, he alone untwists that love from the bidding it has done in sin. Jesus receives her touch in purity because he transforms what she gives. Jesus had come to forgive her of her sins and release her from her bondage to sin. He did not come to make prostitution respectable. He did not say, "You are fine the way you are."

All this makes the Pharisee think something to himself: "If this man were a prophet, he would have known who and what sort of woman this is" (v. 39). Because the Pharisee does not understand grace, he condemns Jesus for prophet-disqualifying conduct. The Pharisee knew that she was a prostitute, and to him, her identity and personhood were entwined with this dangerous sin. But Jesus knew that her sin was not her ontology: being a prostitute may have been *how* she was, but it was not *who* she was. Ontologically speaking, she was an image bearer, a child of God, chosen from before the foundations of the world and set apart for just this moment.

Sin cannot harm Jesus. Not even the sin of those who murdered him could harm him. Satan's greatest attack was God's applied redemption for his children, yielding Satan's final overthrow. Satan thought he triumphed when Jesus was nailed to the cross. But the resurrection of Jesus turned even Satan's titanic violence into crushing defeat. Jesus conquers principalities and powers with contagious grace. God uses even evil to make things good.

Jesus dines with sinners not because sin is no big deal. Jesus dines with sinners not because he expects us to go on sinning. Jesus dines with sinners not because he knows that some of us are just more prone to certain sins than others, and he gives us a free pass when our inclinations lead us into sin. Jesus dines with sinners not because the Roman government made certain sins into a protected class of citizenship. The laws of the land do not nullify the laws of God. Jesus dines with sinners so that he can get close enough to touch us, so that he can participate in the intimacy of table fellowship as a healer and a helper. Jesus comes to change us, to transform us, so that after we have dined with Jesus, we want Jesus more than the sin that beckons our fidelity. And now, in the passage that completes this scene, Jesus rebukes the Pharisee:

> Then turning toward the woman he said to Simon [the Pharisee homeowner], "Do you see this woman? I entered your house; you gave me no water for my feet, but she has wet my feet with her tears and wiped them with her hair. You gave me no kiss, but from the time I came in she has not ceased to kiss my feet. You did not anoint my head with oil, but she has anointed my feet with ointment. Therefore I tell you, her sins, which are many, are forgiven—for she loved much. But he who is forgiven little, loves little." And he said to her, "Your sins are forgiven." Then those who were at table with him began to say among themselves, "Who is this, who even forgives sins?" And he said to the woman, "Your faith has saved you; go in peace." (Luke 9:44–50)

First, Jesus rebukes Simon by reading his mind. That's right. Jesus rebukes Simon for something he thought, not something he said. Next, Jesus rebukes Simon for being a poor host, pointing out that the sinful woman has provided the normal tasks of the hosts: feet washing, warm welcome, ointment for head and feet. Simon has cared for Jesus only instrumentally. He finds Jesus amusing. He wants to hear him teach and then to test him. He has been looking for a good night of apologetic bantering. Simon cares little for Jesus as a man, and his poor manners as a host reveal this.

Second, Jesus does not defend himself from Simon's unspoken rebuke. Instead, he explains the covenant of grace, using the sinful woman as exhibit A. Jesus shows that his forgiveness of her sins is not contingent on her love. Just the opposite. He shows Simon that she loves because he has forgiven her. Her faith is not a work but a posture, a hunger, an openness. Joel Beeke says, "Faith is the empty hand by which we receive Christ and all His benefits."[4]

Christian hospitality is not for sale. It cannot be made into a commodity.

The gospel is free.

Genuine hospitality is not transacted for money. Genuine hospitality does not objectify image bearers and falsify the commandments of God. Genuine hospitality does not gossip and encourage self-aggrandizement. The gospel creates community that welcomes others in. The gospel says to fellow image bearers: "You are welcome here. Come as you are. Take my hand. I'm not leading, I'm following. Jesus is leading."

But how do I know I am following the real Jesus—the Jesus of the Bible—and not the Jesus of my imagination, Jesus my imaginary friend? I know by reading and understanding the Bible as a unified revelation, where Scripture interprets Scripture. Every word of the Bible is a red-letter word. Even the places that take your life captive.

Every day I get up and try to live out the covenant of grace as a public truth in the daily practice of ordinary hospitality.

It isn't always easy.

It begins with recognizing people as your kin.

In the LGBTQ community I belonged to, we developed a keen sense of how to recognize one another. We called it "gay-dar," and over the years we became adept at not just seeing but also recognizing one another.

What is the difference between seeing and recognizing?

Seeing involves catching outward glimpses; recognizing embraces others as your own.

We love because God first loved us.

The love that must stand behind hospitality is covenant love. And covenant love always starts with the fall, because there is no greater example of loving our enemies than God's response to all people after the fall of Adam.

What Is the Covenant, and Why Does It Matter?

The Westminster Larger Catechism asks a simple question: "Did people continue in the state of goodness in which God created us and in which we were destined to dwell before Adam sinned by eating the forbidden fruit?"[5] This is really at the heart of most Christian divisions. Are we born good—or mostly good? Did the fall affect everything, or just some things? Are all who are born after Adam imbued with imputed and inherited depravity? And what exactly was the sin of Adam? Was the fruit bad? Did the fruit make Adam depraved?

No. The fruit was not poison.

The bad was Adam's refusal to obey God's word.

What Is Covenant Love?

Jesus bleeds real blood for all the letters of the Bible, not just the red ones. I may look like an old hippie (and I do), but hospitality gives no cheap love, the kind that says your idols are welcome here, the kind that buys into counterfeit categories of what it means to be human. Idolatry is dangerous—as well as delusional. It miscues our worship, affection, identity, and community. And it is easy—cheap and easy. Who wouldn't prefer embracing a lover you can touch over a God you cannot?

That is why the sharp edges of hospitality ought not to be overlooked: God does not love us just the way we are. God's love is costly, bloody, and powerful. It bore down on the mocking of Satan and the betrayal of friends. His mercy in the Son paid the price of his justice in the Father, and his Spirit forges an irreplaceable, unbreakable, and eternal union with him that carries us through death itself (Psalm 147). This is authentic Christianity, and its steep costs and high yield can be withstood only when the strength of our words matches the strength of our relationships.

These far-reaching things go well with trust and lentil soup, with hot apple cider and fresh bread, with dog walking, child loving, and erranding, with the asking of forgiveness and the seeking of second chances. The fall separated us from God, exposed us to God's curse, revealed the cavernous miseries of life, displayed the eternal pains of hell, and unveiled the new inevitability of death. The fall made us naked. Laughing this off as superstition or declaring on your own steam that "my God wouldn't do that" is fool's poker. Your God—and mine—did do it. We need to stop asking what Jesus our imaginary friend would do and start facing the deep shadow of the cross, because there at the cross we see what Jesus did do and how God provided the way of escape at his expense and for our blessing. But make no mistake: the way is hard. It breaks you. It is best walked in the company of other broken people, accompanying one another in suffering, helping each other repent of sin, bear the cross, and make biblical sense of things.

5

The Gospel Comes with a House Key

The Seal of Hospitality

May 2014, Durham, North Carolina

Kent and I do a lot of public speaking these days. Our Christian neighbors know that we are conservative Christians who appear to run a commune at our house. Sometimes local church pastors invite us to explain what we do in our house and why.

May 8, 2014, under a stunning cloudless Carolina sky, Kent and I gathered up the kids after family devotions and headed to a local Baptist church to give a talk about loving the stranger. Before we left the house, we gave Sally and Bella their treats: red Kongs with frozen peanut butter. I keep a supply in the freezer. We were in a hurry, and we left our Bibles on the table. They were open to the Gospel of Luke. Before I left my house, I looked back. I saw that the Bibles made a rough square on the dining room table, with some Legos and plastic dinosaurs and one light saber. We locked the doors behind us, both the knob and the dead bolt.

Our talk went well, we think. We hope we encouraged other

Christian families to open their homes and see Jesus in those in need. We focused on philoxenia—love for the stranger. This, for Christian audiences, is a hard sell. Christians love to fellowship with like-minded people. Strangers can be another story. We answered good questions about how to develop relationships with people who do not share our class or background. We piled Knox and Mary back into the car and made the hour drive back home, covering familiar territory. It was a good day, and I was looking forward to getting home, making coffee, finishing the laundry, icing my injured foot, and reading the last chapter of *Prince Caspian* to the children.

I knew something was wrong as soon as I walked in the house. My ever-hyper, effervescent, and effusive golden retriever, Sally, was cowering in the corner, hurt and scared. Clothes and dining room plates and family pictures were strewn everywhere. As we walked into the kitchen, we saw it. A window had been snapped at the frame and popped out with a crowbar. The robbers had to stand on the large dog-feeding station to crawl in through the broken window, so obviously they weren't threatened by big dogs. Covering our open Bibles were those things the robbers discarded— some of my mom's china and the golden-colored bowl that Kent uses for baptisms. Seeing the golden baptism bowl next to the Bibles was the only recognizable image in this whole picture.

I looked at my hurt dog and kissed her face. She wagged at me gingerly, but her heart wasn't in it. I walked through the house as if underwater. Sally trailed cautiously behind. The robbers had yanked my mom's television off the wall, leaving holes in the wall and floor, where I suspect they must have dropped it. The drawers to all dressers hung open, and their contents were strewn everywhere: socks, geography puzzle pieces, math videos, marbles, the dog's heart pills. The robbers stole all my jewelry, including my engagement ring, an heirloom that had been in Kent's family for five generations. I always feared I would hurt or lose it if I wore it, especially during summer months, when my hands are deep in garden dirt when they are not holding children or turning book pages or kneading Communion bread. I had stared at it just that morning, contemplating whether it was safe to wear today, and I turned down what turned out to be my last chance.

My mother, who had recently moved to a retirement home, had gifted me with her family jewelry—all of it—for safekeeping and memory's sake. They took it all. My mother had recently been raging because of another family issue—my estranged nephew had reached out to me and not to her, and of course, she discovered this on Facebook. (I'm not on Facebook, or any social media, but the rest of the world is, and that is how she uncovered this.) I was too worn out to even create a strategy for how to tell her what had happened or how to protect myself from her fury. All I could think was: *This is the hand of God. Lean into it.*

The robbers took it all. But the close-range guilt was Sally, my golden, the most extroverted member of our family, who had never been mistreated by anyone except a cat in her whole life. As a golden, she didn't know what *mean* was. Yet there she was— bruised, sad, shivering. When the police came, they explained it like this: big dogs are in the way, and robbers either shoot them or bludgeon them. Sally wasn't shot, and I thanked God for that. The police took our information, fingerprinted every doorknob and doorframe, and left more mess and dirt in their wake.

It was awful to be robbed.

It was ironic to realize that as we advocated for hospitality to the stranger, a stranger beat my dog and walked off with the goods, vandalizing the house just for good measure.

We were all in a state of shock. My children's anxiety rocketed through the roof. Not one of us found *okay* for months.

But that night, when dinnertime rolled around, our people surrounded us. I was not serving but receiving. Our people—our family of God—set the table. Matthew, my dear son in the Lord and an exchange student from Singapore, was scheduled to move into our house that night, as the residence hall at the University of North Carolina was closing for the semester break. It was good to have his calming spirit to help. Susanna was just leaving work and picked up a rotisserie chicken and butter pecan ice cream on her way to our house. She knew I would need butter pecan, so she picked up some Lactaid too.

As is my routine, I moved the prized Kroger chicken from its plastic bed to the pan, and then I gave Sally the plastic container covered in chicken grease and juice. She settled down with it in her favorite posture: nose in the corner and back feet splayed like a water buffalo in yoga (as if she could hide ninety pounds simply by giving us her backside). She held the plastic dish between her paws, and started to perk up when more friends trailed in. Our homeschool dad friends came with tools and Scripture, dropping their lawn care and important executive jobs to help. And after dinner and Bible reading and prayer and a psalm to sing, we started with a bucket and rag, garbage bags, and the vacuum cleaner.

It was hard to be robbed.

It was hard to have God test so powerfully and privately what we proclaimed publicly—that even if you are hurt, people can't take the things that matter most and that will survive to the new heavens and new earth—your soul, his Word, and your someday-glorified body.

The day after we were robbed, Kent pushed the grill to the front yard, where the picnic table was already waiting. Then he posted three things on our Nextdoor app: (1) we were robbed; (2) robbers took stuff, but no one was harmed, and the robbers could not take things of eternal value—the Word of God and the souls of people; (3) we would love for everyone to join us for burgers and hot dogs on the Lord's Day, starting at three o'clock. He pushed "Send." Then Susanna pointed out that Sunday was Mother's Day, and my husband had just invited three hundred people to our front yard. Well, that is how things go at the Butterfields'. Kent also invited our whole church to come. He wanted to make sure that there would be plenty of believers to help our unbelieving neighbors process the robbery. That has always been Kent's strategy—have a house filled with God's people who can then help our neighbors see the hand of God in the everyday details of life, including the providence of being robbed.

It was a joy-filled time, with hot dogs and kids and water guns and meeting new and old friends. Twenty-one neighbors showed up, and most of our church family as well. And when our unbelieving and skeptical neighbors asked how we were holding up, Kent was able to share the gospel with a new legitimacy, because where God is in your loss matters more to a doubting and cynical world than where God is in your plenty.

It was hard to be robbed.

It was awful to come home and find our house ransacked, holes in the walls, underwear touched by the wrong hands, journals and vitamins tossed all over the floor, and the dog we had raised from mitten-size bruised and fearful. It was humiliating to not be sovereign over locked doors and heirloom engagement rings. It ached to take in that he who is sovereign allowed this to happen, for his glory and for my own good (Rom. 8:28).

But it must feel deceptive and sinister to be the people who robbed me. Bad in a way that a coat of paint and the comfort of friends bearing rotisserie chicken and butter pecan ice cream can't fix. It must create a hole in their humanity that they know will someday swallow up everyone they love. When I was sitting at the table, eating our meal and talking and processing what had happened and praying—Bibles open, kids on laps, dogs under feet, feasting on our daily bread, in the midst of a house ransacked by robbers, the chaos of invasion everywhere but the one room in which we gathered—I realized it:

I am blessed.

I am grateful.

I am not the victim.

It was more awful to be my robber than me.

Home as Hospital and Incubator

This idea—that our houses are hospitals and incubators—was something I learned in my lesbian community in New York in the

1990s. We knew that our traditional, so-called Christian neighbors despised and distrusted us and regarded us as abominations. So we set out to be the best neighbors on the block. We gathered in our people close and daily, and we said to each other, "This house, this *habitus*, is a hospital and an incubator. We help each other heal, and we help ideas take root." We duplicated many house keys and made sure that everyone we loved had one. We meant what the key implied: you have access anytime. The door is not meant to hurt you or to keep you away.

This was during the first wave of AIDS, originally called GRID (gay related immune deficiency). Nouns such as *Kaposi's sarcoma*, *toxoplasmosis*, *pneumocystis carinii*, *cytomegalovirus*, *molluscum contagiosum*, *peripheral neuropathy*, and *cryptosporidiosis* went from obscurity to familiar household words. Those were the days when my kitchen window held "Silence = Death" stickers and not children's cutout snowflakes.

The AIDS epidemic required a big learning curve for me and my friends in the lesbian community. Outsiders might not know this, but there is no natural simpatico between women who identify as lesbian and men who identify as gay. We thought our brothers were hedonists, and they thought us politically high-minded prigs. But learn to come together we did. We learned how to care for one another across the fear of the plague. Some of my friends learned how to bootleg AZT before the pharmaceutical companies dropped their prices so that dying people could have a shot at taking it. Out of desperation and fear and banding together in spite of our differences, a community was born. The tenacious, consistent, and sacrificial work of the LGBTQ community—work that was birthed over dinner tables and work benches (like the one I type on right now) have changed the landscape of American culture and pushed the boundaries of natural law. Of that I am sure.[1] I do wonder, now, as a Christian, if the church had been there, had helped, had shared in our grief, how the story would have unfolded differently.

These lessons—learned as far outside the walls of the church as possible—are instructive for Christians. We live in a post-Christian world that is sick and tired of *hearing* from Christians. But who could argue with mercy-driven hospitality? What a potential witness Christians have, untapped and right here at our fingertips.

Christians have a moral responsibility to be good stewards, and this includes stewarding the church, religious liberty, ideas, laws, the family, and the worldwide refugee crisis. The world is watching—and rightly so. And our lack of visible and genuine hospitality—practiced both inside our community and outside—is speaking louder than words right now.

Christians have a powerful history of building schools and hospitals, of showing up during natural disasters to offer water and food and shelter and medicine. We have that history. But do we have the daily witness of Christian neighboring?

Our post-Christian neighbors need to hear and see and taste and feel authentic Christianity, hospitality spreading from every Christian home that includes neighbors in prayer, food, friendship, childcare, dog walking, and all the daily matters upon which friendships are built.

Take, for example, our Christian brothers and sisters who struggle with unchosen homosexual desires and longings, sensibilities and affections, temptations and capacities. Our brothers and sisters need the church to function as the Lord has called it to—as a family. Because Christian conversion always comes in exchange for the life you once loved, not in addition to it, people have much to lose in coming to Christ—and some people have more to lose than others. Some people have one cross, and others have ten to carry. People who live daily with unchosen homosexual desires also live with a host of unanswered questions and unfulfilled life dreams. What is your responsibility to those brothers and sisters who are in this position in life?

One answer is this: the gospel comes with a house key. Mark 10:28–31 reads:

> Peter began to say to [Jesus], "See, we have left everything and followed you." Jesus said, "Truly, I say to you, there is no one who has left house or brothers or sisters or mother or father or

children or lands, for my sake and for the gospel, who will not receive a hundredfold now in this time, houses and brothers and sisters and mothers and children and lands, with persecutions, and in the age to come eternal life."

Please note what Jesus says about how to love anyone who responds to the gospel in faith and obedience and who must lose everything in order to gain the kingdom's promises. Jesus says that he expects we will lose partners and children and houses in the process of conversion, that conversion calls everyone to lose everything. God's people need to wake up to something. If you want to share the gospel with the LGBTQ community or anyone who will lose family and homes, the gospel must come with a house key. This hundredfold blessing promised here in these verses is not going to fall from the sky. It is going to come from the church. It is going to come from the people of God acting like the family of God. God intends this blessing to come from you. And real Christian hospitality that creates real Christian community expresses authentic Christianity in deep and abiding ways to a world that thinks we are hypocrites.

If the gospel comes with a house key, then the people in the house are not primarily instrumentally useful but rather inherently valuable. In Christ we are family. In the family of God the personal is the covenantal, not the political. We—all of us—are image bearers, first and foremost. We belong to each other because we share a heavenly Father. Our identity and our calling must emanate from God's image radiating in and through us.

All around you, people hunger for the covenant of God to include them.

My former neighbor Hank has recently been sentenced to almost two decades in prison, on a plea bargain that turned out to be no bargain at all. He faces a prison sentence potentially longer than his life expectancy. Frequently these days, his letters reveal festering fears that he is homeless, unmoored, unloved, and unwanted, and that if he lives long enough, he will be homeless again upon release. Hank is not just my former neighbor. He very recently put his faith and trust in Jesus. Hank and other prisoners who have committed their lives to Jesus need to know who in the church they will live with when they are released. They need to know where home is.

My oldest daughter, Samantha, was seventeen when we adopted her. I was her eleventh foster mother. She held affiliations with dangerous people when child protective services reclaimed her. And me? I stood in a long line of dysfunctional "mothers." The dysfunctional mother who came right before me adopted her and then sent her back into foster care when she transformed from a perky and mischievous child into a rebellious teenager. Samantha survived a broken adoption at fifteen years old, as well as abuse, neglect, assault, and betrayal. To this day, she is the strongest and most beautiful woman I know. And today, over a decade after our adoption of her, she is estranged from us. Her rejection of us was not intended to harm. We meant her well, and she knows that. We exchange birthday and Christmas cards as well as the occasional text message about our dogs. But she didn't want us to adopt her, even though she needed us to adopt her. We were too little and too late.

So why did we adopt her? Did we have any hope that she would bond with our family? Not really. Our expectations were pretty sensible. We adopted Samantha because we believed, to the best of our ability to do so, that God was calling us to do it. We did not adopt her because we wanted something in return. I remember the stares and the facial expressions of some nice churchy types when we said we were adopting a troubled teenager. With heads cocked, cold hearts, and sarcasm insulated by enough pride to choke a horse, they uttered: "Well, these kind of things never work out, but I hope it works out for you." My only reply was the obvious: "It already did work out."

We loved Samantha from the minute we met her, and we wanted her to have a home from which to launch. Sometimes people need homes to nest in, and sometimes people need homes to launch from. Both are crucial. Both are God's work. Sometimes people ask if it "worked out" to adopt Samantha, with all her problems and all the barriers to connection we had. Samantha moved out as fast as she could, reconnected with her birth family, and moved on and away from us. Did it work out? Yes. Kent and I obeyed God. The gospel comes with a house key, not because it is easy, but because it is hard. God makes the key—and the lock to fit it.

Thanksgiving 2016: Making Room

We had twenty-seven church friends and neighbors and family join us for our meal and fellowship this past Thanksgiving. It took some planning, but the children, Kent, and I managed to find a way to serve twenty-seven people comfortably. My neighbor Donna helped. She is ingenious and owns many tablecloths. One of the ladies from the back-porch Bible group lent me thirty matching wine glasses. Our "dining room" was three rooms opened together, with a small table in the foyer for very young children. Sitting arrangements are simple: those over fifty can assume they will have a chair with a back. Those over twenty and with children can assume they will have a table to place their plate on. Teens and children are encouraged to use their creativity. Our large group gathers for prayer, hand over hand, circling through rooms and around dogs. After the blessings, the older folks find a seat at the table. The children pile their Corelle plates high and head out to the fort or the trampoline or the back porch to eat in peace.

This setup became so practical that we have kept the house in this hospitality-ready position ever since. Everyone knows the routine. With good Carolina weather and forts and hammocks and a trampoline and a back porch, our dinner gatherings gather big and spill over easily, a dinner bell calling the children, big and little, back for Bible devotions and dessert.

One of the people who blesses our table is our brother in the Lord, Zion. Zion worships with us every other week, and his sponsor for such highly supervised outings is a member of our church. During some visits, a prison guard also shows up, just to make sure that Zion is where he is supposed to be. Zion is serving out the last two years of a decade-long sentence in a low-security prison in a neighboring county. Zion also comes to our home on all holidays. He is allowed out of the prison walls for only five hours every other week. We aim to make those five hours precious.

Zion sat next to me at dinner. He was unusually quiet, subdued. He had tears bubbling in his eyes. We passed the potatoes, and his eyes locked mine, and he said: "I've never been in a home before. I mean, it's been a long time. No. never. I've never been in a home. Not like this. With love. With Christ. With brothers and sisters. With children. And I belong too. Here." He had been in my home before, so I wasn't quite tracking, but something was triggering something big. I took his hand in mine. As Zion spoke, it all spilled out. So many broken promises. So many loved ones lost. Insurmountable collateral damage. Impossible to see the way forward, except by the grace of God.

As I listened, I caught a glimpse of my son Michael with one arm around his young wife and his just-turned-one-year-old son perched on his strong and able shoulders. Adopted at seventeen, it has taken him this many years to receive this table as his own as well. After all, we don't look like each other. We don't share personal history. The betrayals he has faced go deep. I don't understand any of this in my flesh. But my soul gets it, only because of Christ's bloody love. Only in Christ do we share covenantal history and kingly futures. And somehow, at the table, we belong to each other, believer and unbeliever coming together under God's authority. God's authority makes us loving. We are family.

The gospel comes with a house key. When table fellowship includes those from prison, orphanhood, and poverty in real and abiding ways, permanent bonds of care and kinship are the consequence. We belong to each other, and even though we may have just realized it, we always have.

We live in a world that heartlessly accepts as normal a worldwide refugee crisis, a world that has grown numb to the increasing numbers of children "aging out" of foster care and into homelessness, a world that accepts insanely long terms of incarceration for nonviolent crimes. Often, we Christians have no idea how to open our hearts and our homes to include people who need to be there. We love the miraculous stories of Jesus, his feeding of the five thousand, his divine healing, his contagious grace. And we miss the most obvious things about these stories: that we are meant to replicate them in ordinary, nonmiraculous ways. This is what it means to call people to see themselves in God's image and to live within the covenant of grace:

> The distance between God and the creature is so great that although reasonable creatures do owe obedience unto him as their Creator, yet they could never have any fruition of him as their blessedness and reward, but by some voluntary conde-scension on God's part, which he hath been pleased to express by way of covenant.[2]

The distance between God and his creatures after the fall is insurmountable. The imputation of Adam's sin rages on, pitting man against man, man against God, and man against his own conscience. Hospitality is the obvious bridge that brings desperate people into a Christian home, where they can both receive and give great blessings. Christians know the difference between giving grace and putting a millstone around someone's neck. What is the difference? Grace is bloody. Grace is purchased by the blood of Christ. Grace brings you to your knees. Grace gives you safety to repent. A millstone encourages you to sin against God and others all in the name of being kind to the weakness of the flesh. Hospitality brings you into a daily need to have a plan for sin—yours and other people's. Desperate people do desperate things. But the question is: Do Christian people practice Christian hospitality in regular, ordinary, consistent ways? Or do we think our homes too precious for criminals and outcasts? Our homes are not our castles. Indeed, they are not even ours.

So where can you start? Start where you are.

Short-Term and Dependable Hospitality in the Home

We have learned that our home is equipped for regular, short-term, live-in ministry needs. We have a room in the basement with a bed and a desk (good for adults or even families, if we add extra air mattresses). Our two youngest children are now eleven and fourteen. They willingly give up bedrooms and take their sleeping bags to the living room, leaving two bedrooms open for children in need. We anticipate that people we know from our church (singles going through stressful times or families who have temporarily lost housing) or children or families we know from SAFE families will need our home.[3]

A decade ago, we lived in Virginia, and we were a licensed foster family. We changed everything in our home so that children in need could be safe. We moved the Windex and Clorox from under the sink to a cabinet way over my head. We put plugs in every electric outlet. We had baby monitors next to the crib and baby gates at the top of the stairs. We lived this way long after someone whose last name was Butterfield benefited.

And so too today, we see our home as a palette of color and hope, of comfort and restoration, of God's healing and grace, for someone we do not yet know, or for someone we do know and whose living situation has become untenable. This is all very basic.

Sometimes it is just a matter of listening well to your friends.

My friend Susanna was scheduled for eye surgery. A single and fiercely independent woman, she thought she was going to Uber her way to the hospital and back, get up the next morning pain-free and fully functioning, and go on with life, business as usual. I busted her bubble and showed up at the eye clinic, sans kids, with a pile of books and a bag of knitting. Books and knitting signaled that I was there for the long haul and there was no getting rid of me. And after surgery, I guided my valium-pumped, semi-blind friend home to recover at our house. Her housemate drove halfway to our house to give me her overnight bag so my friend could have her own toothbrush and pj's and extra clothes. Recovery was painful. Although she stubbornly refused to take anything more than Tylenol for the pain, Kent drove in a snowstorm to fill the script for all narcotics offered so we could have them on hand. The doc had said that the pain on the second day would be so severe that it would feel like labor pain in her eyeballs. Kent and I don't know experientially what that analogy means, but we know that when doctors say such things, it means very, very bad pain.

Susanna is one of the strongest women I know. She is a trooper. Her eyes throbbed. She couldn't see. She couldn't bear any light. She rested and slept a lot. She applied drops every three hours. Our family made sure that she had rest, good food, clean laundry, and transportation to follow-up appointments. We turned off all the lights and drew all the shades. All for one and one for all. None of this was hard.

On the third day, at breakfast, Susanna was feeling better. But she still wasn't seeing well, and that was starting to be scary. I knew she was really discouraged by the length of the recovery, especially given her expectations. After a bite of eggs, she put down her fork and asked me a question: "Where does all the magic here come from?" Her question came as she looked at the table, her hand sweeping its expanse, taking in the scrambled eggs and toast and fruit and the unfolded laundry on the table in the homeschool room, the kids giggling over something in the other room, Kent reading his Bible in his chair. It was a question that came from a thankful and inquiring heart. And it is a very important question. Where does the day-to-day momentum that feeds, nurtures, and heals, that holds a household together, that invites others to come in and rest and recover, that says yes more than no—where does this momentum come from?

The answer that casts the widest net is God. God makes the magic. And God can make magic in all kinds of faithful households—those run by single Christians and those run by married Christians. But there are particulars about our house, particulars that most of my feminist friends find offensive. The particulars that make up the magic in my house have something to do with the sacrifices we have made so that I can be a stay-at-home mom, something about the particular dynamics of a husband and a wife who love Jesus most of all and who value hospitality in a daily way.

The ingredients of this magic are commonplace, found in the book of Genesis. The family, by God's design, fulfills the creation mandate, and God blesses the nurturing that comes from it. In the family, God starts with a dad who is head of his household, who rules by God's love and law. He takes care of his family. He provides. He shepherds well, according to the Bible. He is not an ogre or a bully or an angry boss. He leads in teaching his family to apply the means of God's grace to all tasks. He understands that grace always brings people into God's protection, not away from it. So he models the hard things about biblical living as well as the comfortable.

Next in the biblical family is a mom who is home and available to serve. While I am employable in a full-time way outside the home, our family has always needed me at home, and so home I am. As a stay-at-home mom I can do one hundred helpful things for the people I love most in the world in the first thirty minutes of waking. Things that matter cannot be farmed out to others for pay. I love my role as Kent's helper and the mother of our children and the general cook for this house that serves, feeds, and nourishes our family of God and our neighbors.

The comfort comes from our covenantal God, who knows what we need and who places a dad who knows how to be a leader and a mom who submits to a godly husband in the covenant of marriage. And in the balance of this one-flesh union, as husband and wife cleave and nurture each other and their children, they simultaneously reverberate this nurturing capacity to others. But make no mistake: this magic comes from a mom and a dad who put Christ at the center of the home and make the sacrifices necessary to value keeping a home over keeping afloat a two-family career.

As I write these words, I know I tread on thin ice.

I came to this idea with nothing short of wild grief. How could the sacrifice that blesses our family and community most be the social norm that I battled fiercely against for the most formative years of my young adult life? Does anyone else believe this? If I had a dollar for everyone who has told me (both inside and outside the church) that I am wasting my education by staying at home and caring for my children, I would be a rich woman.

When I told Susanna that the magic comes from a stay-at-home mom and a dad who takes his leadership seriously, she almost choked on her scrambled eggs. (I understand. God knows I am traveling on what feels like enemy territory too.) But eat her eggs she did and, alas, became complicit with me in the very same "patriarchy" that we were both trained to despise.

The godly submission of a faithful wife to her head—her husband—does not diminish the power and strength that God has given to women but instead channels it to serve the most important people first. It was a hard pill to swallow, but I have come to learn that godly patriarchy is not my enemy—or the enemy of any woman. Godly patriarchy means rule by the godly fathers, the good men who sacrifice their lives for the protection of their family. In God's hands, when the good fathers lead, the roaming gangs of violent men are kept in check and away. We need godly patriarchs because sin is real, and the droving gangs of male violence are real too. If men aren't trained to lead by God's design, they often destroy by Satan's command.

There are many other vital ways to run a hospitality house, and singles are just as good and capable as married people. But the magic in this house comes from the particulars in this house. And it starts here with a husband who shepherds well in response to the call that Christ put on him.[4]

And what about the people who have been nurtured and fed at my table? They have left my table to conquer the world again and again and again. I'm honored to play the behind-the-scenes role of table fellowship, of food and prayer, nursemaid and launderer, seamstress and coach. And the Lord has also given me, at different seasons, work that brings me before wider audiences, like writing this book. But do not be deceived: home is where the magic is. And the kitchen is my kingdom.

Lisa

> Older women likewise are to be reverent in behavior, not
> slanderers or slaves to much wine. They are to teach what is
> good, and so train the young women to love their husbands
> and children, to be self-controlled, pure, working at home,
> kind, and submissive to their own husbands, that the word
> of God may not be reviled. (Titus 2:3–5)

Life outside of Christ is infantilizing. It celebrates youth, and it revels in irresponsibility. It values self-indulgence, not self-control. I was surprised to realize upon conversion that I was in the Titus 2 category of older woman. I had missed key developmental stages of womanhood in the ignorance and indulgence of sin and unbelief. I came to my senses with grief as well as with purpose.

Part of my Titus 2 ministry to young, single women involves helping them do "what is good" as they keep their hands to the plow during the final stages of graduate school. Those final miles are rigorous and defeating. They break you in ways that only the initiated understand. An older woman has an important role to play in the life of a young Christian woman finishing graduate school. She can hold up her arms in prayer, and offer both the spiritual and material support needed to finish strong. She can hold up a mirror. She can offer rebalancing as needed, for graduate programs are always discipling programs, and any form of discipleship that does not have Christ as its center holds pitfalls and dangers, things that older godly women who have walked this road can understand.

It is not sinful or wrong for women to prepare themselves for professional work that demands the highest level of academic preparation. Women, even women who feel called to marriage, must prepare for how they will take care of themselves if the Lord does not call them to marriage. Christian women must study hard and well and apply themselves to the rigors of professional training. And just as young, married women and young mothers need older women in the church to come alongside them and provide prayer and guidance and support and counsel, so, too, young women in graduate school and professional women need older women in the church to come alongside them and provide prayer and guidance and support and counsel. Edgy and smart women are vital to the church, yet often the church has no idea how to help them in the shattering ordeal of graduate training.

Lisa joined our church during her medical school training, during the hardest and most frightening season of her life. Each day of medical school brought her to the brink of terror. She comes from a family of modest means. She is a trailblazer and the title holder of a lot of family firsts: first woman to graduate top of her class, first woman to go to graduate school, and, soon, first woman to hold the title "Dr."

During medical school she struggled with sleep deprivation and imposter identity, as she was daily surrounded by people in her medical program who came with social privilege. Her supervising professor was ruthlessly hard on her. Her anxiety was bullying her. She felt immobilized by fear. She had stopped eating. Self-harm was just one way to keep herself awake, and it was right around the corner. How did I know she needed help? I didn't. She did. I just asked the question.

After church one day, I noticed the telltale signs. She looked just like I did in graduate school. I knew the terror. I knew the prison house of self-harm. And so I did the obvious. I said, "Can I be of some earthly good to you as you finish up this crazy program? Pack your lunch? Do your laundry? Do you want to move in? I can fold your socks while you slay the dragon. What do you think?"

The following week I received a text message that said, "Can you help me?" I texted back: "Of course! What do you need?" Lisa texted: "Food! Rice and dhal and Kevita water."

I was in the middle of making bread for Communion, and my friend Susanna was at my house. It was Saturday, late afternoon, and she and my daughter Mary had just returned from a Compassion International event with renewed commitment to write to their sponsored children. Susanna left her unfinished letter to deliver a meal box to Lisa, but when she got to Lisa, she knew that she needed more than a meal. Susanna texted me, and I texted Lisa and asked her to move into our home for the remaining month of her hellish practicum. She moved in that hour.

For the following month Lisa folded into the general care and rhythm of our house. Often when I was up at four o'clock to work on this book, Lisa was already at the kitchen table studying or sleeping crumpled in a pile of books and notes. I made coffee, and we talked and prayed and packed her lunch.

During the course of her month here, we fed her and did her laundry and listened and prayed. Same channel, same story. Nothing about that month was hard for us. The *hard* was all on Lisa.

The final homestretch was a bear, and she had been surviving on three or four hours of sleep each night for so long that she'd forgotten what REM feels like. I observed her working at the kitchen table one evening, and I immediately took the reading glasses off the top of my head and gave them to her. They helped. Kent tried to get the extra computer screen to work so that Lisa could benefit from two screens as she studied. We moved the Fit Desk to where she could access it best so she could move around some as she toiled.

We fell into a routine. In the dark of morning, when all sane people sleep, Lisa would give me a list of things to pray for as the long day proceeded. I prayed that God's providence would lighten her case load, that her supervisor would be kind, that she would find joy in caring for her patients, that the Lord would give her success. As God answered prayer throughout the day, Lisa would text me so that we could celebrate. At dinner Kent and I were there to process setbacks and job offers.

And then Lisa crossed the finish line, graduated, and moved out. It was a crucial—and short—season of her life. We didn't do anything unusual. We opened our arms wide. We folded Lisa in to the love and care of our home, watched her work, supported her with prayer and caregiving, and celebrated with her when she finished her program. We were glad to help. We were inspired to see the Lord lead her out of the valley of the shadow of death.

Let Perfect Love Cast out Fear

We sometimes fear that our neighbors will bring into our homes problems and issues that we are not ready to discuss in front of our children. We pit the command to nurture and teach our children in the fear and admonition of the Lord against the command to love our neighbor.

We must stop and think this through. On the one hand, we of course must protect our children from harm. On the other hand, we must not presume that sheltering them will accomplish this. Perhaps our children need to know that when they confront doubts and fears, sexual temptations, and moral and faith crises, we will not be shocked, offended, or hurt by this reality.

Our children need to know that we know how serious the Enemy is, how alien and powerful our righteousness in Christ is, and how deep and wide and big and powerful our sin can become if we hide it.

But if we have a ministry to the lost, and if our children know that we truly love our unbelieving neighbors, if they have witnessed us coming alongside those who are struggling or burdened or falling under the weight of sin and tragedy, perhaps, just perhaps, our children will trust us with their deep things. Perhaps they will remember that we embraced our neighbors and strangers, that we loved them and prayed for them, and that we were not jostled or unsettled to share block parties or BBQs, our churches and our homes, with troubled people. Perhaps our love of those image bearers, all of them, especially the difficult ones, will be a pledge to our children that the mosaics of their private lives are safe with us.

We had a chance to live this out when our neighbor Hank was arrested for making crystal meth in his garage. Hank had been our friend. My son Knox especially connected with Hank's love of nature, his ability to fix anything, his attention to detail, and his concern for our safety on long hikes. When Hank was arrested, our house, both because of its proximity to Hank's and because of our friendship, became a Red Cross for complaining neighbors. With sadness, we realized that we were the only neighbors who actually saw Hank as a human being, made in the image of God. Knox was brokenhearted at Hank's situation—all of it, the way it betrayed us and the way it made us fear for his life. Knox was also brokenhearted by the way our neighbors talked about Hank. He observed, "They talk about Mr. Hank like he is an animal or an alien creature." I was simply unable to comfort my son. So I sent a text to Uncle Christopher.

Uncle Christopher is my friend Christopher Yuan, coauthor of *Out of a Far Country*.[5] Christopher and Leon and Angela Yuan are uncle, Nai Nai (Grandma), and Ye Ye (Grandpa) to my children. The Yuans are our family. And Christopher served time in federal prison for dealing crystal meth. He was the perfect friend and counselor and uncle in the Lord for my sensitive son.

Knox and Uncle Christopher talked and texted frequently during the days that followed Hank's arrest. And after that, Knox daily prayed for Mr. Hank, that he would have a cell just like Uncle Christopher's, with "Bible verses on the wall." (Truth be told, there was one Bible verse written on Christopher's cell wall and a whole lot of other things that were not very God honoring. But Knox latched on to this one detail, so this is how he prayed.)

That relationship with Christopher was a touchstone for my son. It communicated this: Mr. Hank may be lost to us, but he is not lost to God. Mr. Hank is in good hands, even now. That relationship has continued to grow over time and through other circumstances. It is good for children to have many Christian adults pouring into their lives, helping them apply faith to the facts of a hard situation.

Be a Way of Escape for Someone—Live as Living Epistles

Radically ordinary hospitality begins when we remember that God uses us as living epistles and that the openness or inaccessibility of our homes and hearts stands between life and death, victory and defeat, and grace or shame for most people.

Consider with me the tension of 1 Corinthians 10:13: "No temptation has overtaken you that is not common to man. God is faithful, and he will not let you be tempted beyond your ability, but with the temptation he will also provide the way of escape, that you may be able to endure it." This passage speaks to the intensity, the loneliness, and the danger of temptation. It also speaks to the lived tension of applying faith to our trials and then waiting for that way of escape to present itself. Have you ever thought that you, your house, and your time are not your own but rather God's ordained way of escape for someone?

I think about this every Lord's Day morning as I am preparing food for two meals: one weekly fellowship meal at church and one meal at home with neighbors and friends and folks from church. I pray as I prepare food, remembering how the Lord's Day was a special day of temptation for me when I was a new believer. You see, beyond its wholesome surface, it is a day of warfare *in toto*. Perhaps you have not noticed this, but the Lord's Day is a terrible day of temptation and sin for many people. Without the moorings of worship, a vital church community, and meaningful fellowship, it is nearly impossible to actually honor the fourth commandment—the commandment that reminds us to "remember the Sabbath day, to keep it holy" (Ex. 20:8).

How do we "remember" this, what we now call the "Lord's Day"? The best way to remember anything is to do it collectively. God is calling me to remember the Lord's Day not just for myself, for my own personal holiness, but also to live in such a way that I enable others to do so as well. I am called to create a place at the table for others, to be available to the hurting and the lost.

We keep the Lord's Day in this communal way by sharing the ordinary means of grace that God has given to us. The Lord's Day is not "family day" or "just us day." If you preserve this day in that way, you steal glory from God and unwittingly cause others to stumble. Remember 1 Corinthians 10:13? You are the way of escape.

Living in community is not just pleasant; it is life saving. In *Life Together* Bonhoeffer comments:

> Sin demands to have a man by himself. It withdraws him from the community. The more isolated a person is, the more extrac-

tive will be the power of sin over him, and the more deeply he becomes involved in it, the more disastrous is his isolation.[6]

Sin demands isolation. While community does not inoculate us against sin, godly community is a sweet balm of safety. It gives us a place and a season where we are safe with ourselves and safe with others.

My favorite day of the week is the Lord's Day, and I want to share that day with others. Kent and I open our home after worship to anyone who will come. We must. We remember what it is like to be a new Christian, to be single, to have secrets that get you alone and torment you, and to have no place to go after worship, the odd tearing apart of the body of Christ as each retreats to her own corner or clique while the benediction still rings in the air. It is an act of violence and cruelty to people in your church who routinely have no place to belong, no place to need and be needed, after worship. Worship leaves us full and raw, and we need one another.

We live in a world that highly values functionality. But there is such a thing as being too functional. When we are too functional, we forget that the Christian life is a calling, not a performance. Hospitality is necessary whether you have cat hair on the couch or not. People will die of chronic loneliness sooner than they will cat hair in the soup.

Know that someone is spared another spiral binge of pornography because he is instead playing Connect Four with you or walking the dogs or jumping on the trampoline. Know that these small things that you may take for granted have been the Lord's appointed way of escape for a brother or sister. Know that someone is spared the fear and darkness of depression because she is needed at your house, always on the Lord's Day, the day she is never alone but instead safely in community where her place at the table is needed and necessary and relied upon.

Know that someone is drawn into Christ's love because the Bible reading and singing that come at the close of the meal include everyone, and it reminds us that no one is scapegoated in this Christ-bearing community.

Safe Families

Open the doors of the covenant community wide and then toss over your shoulders and carry home someone who cannot walk there herself. Have you ever considered becoming a licensed foster family or a host with SAFE Families for Children?[7] When you become licensed to bring into your home people you would never even know about without agency mediation, you have access to children and families in need. Becoming licensed does not force you to take on children or problems that exceed your capacity. But it does give you access to people in need. You can always bring people to the throne of grace even if you cannot bring them home.

If many families in the church work within the foster system or the SAFE Family network, you can resource one another in vital ways. Single Christians have a life-giving role to play in this. There are many teenagers in the foster care system who will be placed only in single-sexed homes because of a history of sexual abuse. There are single Christians in your church called to foster parenting who need the support of other families in the church to take up some of the burden of single parenting and answer this call. There are too many teenagers in foster care, waiting for the adult mentors they need to help them in all transitions in life. Single Christians may be uniquely called to step into the lives of teenagers in foster care, to turn a pivotal crisis into a powerful victory.

Even if adopting or foster parenting is not your calling, you may be able to train as a big brother or a big sister or become a guardian *ad litem*. Perhaps you can partner with another family in the church to keep a sibling group together, or use your training to provide respite care for a church family with special-needs children. If you work with the SAFE Families program, perhaps church members who live closely can all care for a family rendered homeless because of poverty or job loss or flooding. You can work together to get these friends you have not yet met back on their feet.

Recently Kent and I and others from our church attended a SAFE Families orientation meeting. As Chloe, the community leader, was discussing how life preserving it is to resource families and how Christians are called to help keep families together, a little boy ran crying into the room. He was part of a SAFE Families placement. His mom and dad were getting the job training they needed to keep their jobs, but his house had been flooded, and the family was separated. The department of family services referred this case to SAFE Families, because they are overwhelmed with children in need. This little boy was a good SAFE Families fit because the need was short-term (three to six months), and the cause of the crisis was circumstantial (flooding that destroyed the family home), not addiction or violence. The three-year-old boy had fallen on the playground, and the playground worker had opened the door into the meeting hall. Without a beat, the boy made a beeline to his SAFE family, threw himself into the mom's arms, and received a cool drink, a cool washcloth, some Bactine, and a Band-Aid. He had known his SAFE Families mom for a month, but that didn't matter. He knew where to go. The room shattered in tears. A Christian family that had been SAFE Families–approved had open arms, and a little boy with a skinned knee will have no idea what terrors God spared him because of this. But his parents, who love him but could not care for him for reasons beyond their control, could appreciate the danger and the way of escape. This could be a lifelong relationship. Could you be that home?

Just yesterday we received an email that the boy is being reunited with his mom and dad, and they are moving into a new apartment with secure jobs. SAFE Families allows Christians to help those people we would never know without agency mediation. It is an accessible place to start if you want to know how to meet people outside of your social class or neighborhood.

Solve the Big Problems

God wants you to help solve the big problems too.

> You own a house or rent an apartment. You live with your family or by yourself. You wake in the morning and drink your coffee or tea. You drive a car or a motorbike, or perhaps you take the bus. You go to work and turn on your computer. . . . You have hopes, dreams, and expectations. You take your humanity for granted. You keep believing you are human even when the catastrophe arrives and renders you homeless. Your town is in ruins. You try to make it to the border. Only then, hoping to leave, or making it across the border, do you understand that those who live on the other side do not see you as human at all. This is the dread experience of becoming a refugee, or joining the 65 million unwanted and stateless people in the world today.[8]

We live amidst a worldwide refugee crisis, the worst this world has seen since World War II. The UN Refugee Agency (UNHCR) noted that illegal border crossings increased by 277 percent in 2014—many illegal crossings made by orphans. The experience is harrowing:

> UNHCR estimates that 170,000 made it to Europe via the central Mediterranean . . . while 24,000 children arrived by sea just in Italy and Malta, more than half unaccompanied. Each of these thousands of people typically spends one to four days on the high seas on severely overcrowded, unseaworthy boats in the hands of criminal smugglers with no food, water, or even life preservers. Boats have been stranded for as long as two weeks, have capsized, sunk, suffered fires, been maliciously rammed by other vessels, and are routinely abandoned at sea by traffickers.[9]

Who should take responsibility for this global humanitarian crisis?

Is it safe to get involved?

Are refugees terrorists?

Is it responsible to use the Bible to guide our actions?

These are hard and good questions. But one thing is clear: desperate people do desperate things. Christians are not called to be desperate people, even in desperate times. The psalms bear witness to this. Christians are called to do God's work in desperate times.

It is deadly to ignore biblical teaching about serving the stranger—deadly to the people who desperately need help and deadly to anyone who claims Christ as King. Membership in the kingdom of God is intimately linked to the practice of hospitality in this life. Hospitality is the ground zero of the Christian life, biblically speaking. A more crucial question for the Bible-believing Christian is this: Is it safe to fail to get involved?

Jesus says, "I was hungry and you gave me food, I was thirsty and you gave me drink, I was a stranger and you welcomed me, I was naked and you clothed me, I was sick and you visited me, I was in prison and you came to me" (Matt. 25:35–36). When we feel entitled to God's grace, either because of our family history or our decision making, we can never get to the core sentiment behind Jesus's words. What would it take to see Jesus as he portrays himself here? To see ourselves? Is our lack of care for the refugee and the stranger an innocent lack of opportunity, or is it a form of willful violence? Is it a reasonable act of self-preservation, or is it obdurate sin?[10]

American poet William Stafford (1914–1993), in his poem "Easter Morning," defines an encounter with Jesus this way: "You just shiver alive and are left standing / there suddenly brought to account: saved." Stafford then portrays the challenge of discerning Jesus in the stranger, because sometimes you open the door and get Satan instead. He writes: "The slick voice can sell you anything, even / Hell, which is what you're getting by listening."

The risk is laid bare: when we fail to see Jesus in others, we cheapen the power of the image of God to shine over the darkness of the world. When we always see him in others, we fail to discern that we live in a fallen world, one in which Satan knows where we live. Discernment doesn't build walls, however. Discernment doesn't renege on our command by God to practice hospitality.

Practicing Radically Ordinary Hospitality Is Good for the Giver

We have so many barriers to practicing hospitality in the one place that it is vitally and daily needed: the Christian home. We fear that we will not measure up, that we are failing to protect our children in this dangerous world, that we will get in over our heads with people and their needs, and that they will suck us dry in the process. We know that God commands us to practice hospitality for his glory and for the protection of fellow image bearers, but in what way is the practice of radically ordinary hospitality commanded for the good of the giver?

Practicing radically ordinary hospitality helps us keep a guard over our mouth (Ps. 141:3) and learn how to speak only words of grace that build others up in Christ: "Let no corrupting talk come out of your mouths, but only such as is good for building up, as fits the occasion, that it may give grace to those who hear" (Eph. 4:29). We live with a powerful draught of bloody, faithful grace, given freely but in a manner that was agonizingly costly by Christ and bestowed on us for our union with Christ, our sanctification through Christ, and the communion of the saints.

As people gather around your table, Christ heals the parched lands of their hearts as you share words of salt and light, informally spilling into the needs of the moment with humility, patience, gentleness, and open Bibles. Radically ordinary hospitality means silence and sadness turn into prayer without "calling for prayer requests." It happens when Bibles flip open as tension or division escalates, not to avoid the conflict, but to ask Jesus to enter it.

Because it is not "just us" here, because you have chosen company with hurting people who have your house key, you are not going to let your guard down. This, by God's grace, will not be a day that turns into a night of torment, as you replay what you said and wish you could erase it. Your children are learning how to live and share the gospel with fluency and how to love it before a watching world. And you see gospel fruit in your role in God's community as a healer and helper, as a server and caregiver, as a receiver and needer. You have sharpened your prayers with heartache over people you would never know without a hospitable home. You count it joy—even when you are dead tired—knowing that God will magnify your efforts.

Learning how to practice mercy in a world that values covetousness, achievement, and acquisition takes some training, both in learning the new and unlearning the useless. We live in a world that is in great need of the Jesus paradox, of contagious grace, and conservative Christians are poised to serve in ways we have not yet done before.

But what about Judas Iscariot? Does he get a house key too?

6

Judas in the Church

The Borderland of Hospitality

August 2014, Lord's Day Afternoon, Butterfield House

The house was bustling with friends from church and the neighborhood, all migrating into the dining room for our evening Lord's Day meal. After worship, this is the part that I look forward to most. That day we were filling all three tables with church family and neighbors.

We passed plates, and I refilled glasses of iced tea. An odd reality of life in the South is that people request ice with every drink, during all seasons. It clinks like mismatched chimes. And keeping ice from melting in the summer South is simply a scientific impossibility. But the fruitless attempts are part of what makes southerners feel at home. So I set the ice bucket aside to refill and helped the older members of our church to sit first.

As I leaned over to pour a refill of sweet tea into the sweating glass of Mr. Buzzy, he looked up at me, eyes warm and loving, and then, with no malice or intent to do harm, dropped this bomb: "Rosaria, I just realized something. You are just like Rex Miller."

He smiled wide, like he had just delivered my birthday flowers.

"You both sinned. Big time. And you both repented. Publicly. That's pretty cool! I praise God for you both."

He meant no guile. He intended no harm. And he was theologically dead right and accurate. He said it in love. He meant it in love.

And I wanted to receive his observation in the manner in which he intended it. In love. But my pride welled up like acid reflux. Preposterous, I thought! How could I be like Rex?

We were—as we almost always are around here—a politically mixed group. Unbelieving neighbors and church members all together.

Not everyone at my table that day believed that homosexuality is a sin, and therefore linking my past with a recently arrested sex criminal was more than some people could bear. A neighbor who knew my sexual history caught my eye, searching me for a response. That analogy between homosexuality and sex crimes had been worn to a pulp in recent political discussion about gay marriage. And here it was, rising up at my dinner table. My pride is still reinvigorated when I let my guard down to defend the person I used to be. Deep inside, ever since the public sin of Rex Miller blew wide open, all over the news, all over the community, I believed that I was different from Rex. Better.

Publicly linking Mary Magdalene the pastor's wife with the church-disciplined and now incarcerated sex offender de-horsed all conversation.

It was awkward with a capital A—for me and everybody else.

The room quieted.

Many different kinds of faces looked at me. Wounded faces. Upset faces. Sympathetic faces. Embarrassed faces. Uncertain faces.

This felt like public humiliation, and it made me rethink this whole practice of daily, rhythm-of-life hospitality, with competing worldviews at the same table. It made me scramble for a safety net. It made me wonder if this practice of open invitations was a good one. Maybe it would be safer if I looked through the church directory and invited only the people who saw things eye to eye? Maybe a little civilized compartmentalization according to world-view peace is what our house needed?

However, radically ordinary Christian hospitality does not happen in La La Land. It's gritty and messy, and it forces us to deal with diversity and difference of opinion, with difficult people, with our own unrepented sin and hard hearts. It demands forgiveness before any of us is ready to cough it up.

Here is the backstory to my Awkward-with-a-capital-A moment.

Rex Miller was the subject of a very public scandal and arrest for child pornography. His case was all over the news, and this went on for months on end. Real names. Real faces. While in jail, he pleaded guilty and agreed to a plea bargain. Rex repented of his sin and took the full measure of the punishment, never defending himself and never asking for a lesser punishment. He is older and in ill-health. His long-suffering family stayed by his side, which is no picnic.

After the case broke and prior to his incarceration, he received counseling from Kent and the elders; he was removed from the Lord's Supper as part of his church discipline. To be sure, the civil magistrate's discipline overshadowed the church's. But to Rex's immediate family and to the body of Christ, all of this was palpable and painful.

At the very same time Ben Little, a church elder, was caught in adultery. He took a different route than Rex, defending, excusing, and pointing fingers at everyone else. Ben was immediately removed as an elder in the church. Unlike Rex, who repented, Ben continued the spiral-downward fall. He divorced his infirm and faithful wife. He blame shifted. He continued living in sin. After years of counseling and pleading and praying, Ben was excommunicated. He left our church, and many of us never saw or heard from him again.

Sexual sin did both men in.

One repented behind bars; the other refused.

Our church and our community have been struggling with the consequence of these two church discipline cases ever since.

And there at my dinner table, the sudden mixing of church discipline with hospitality was oil on water, or gasoline on a flame.

Adding to the pain of the moment was who both men had been before their public fall.

Both men had held socially conservative positions with a strong and strident edge. They had talked about the prospect of gay marriage and about people who identified and lived as gay and lesbian or transgender as if these were not our neighbors and as if we were not still talking about fellow image bearers of God. They talked about the LGBTQ community as if I and other genuine followers of Christ hadn't immigrated from the other side of this fence. It was excruciating.

Both men had presented themselves as great family men—upstanding fathers and husbands. They'd put on a good show. They'd looked like the real deal. Except that they weren't.

Both men had also had legitimate ministries. One was an amazing teacher, the other an avid reader. They had touched our lives—all our lives. We had shared good times together, and we had looked forward to more. One served us Communion, and the other organized church-sponsored camping trips and cookouts. Their gifts were real. We lost something vital when we lost them to sin.

Kent announced both discipline cases on the same Lord's Day. It was a grand slam of shame for all of us.

Sexual sin has ravaged our little local church.

Sexual sin is ravaging the church universal.

Sometimes when sexual sin plunders the church, we feel ill and outraged.

Other times when sexual sin razes the church, we feel smugly entitled and secretly proud to be on the "right side of history."

Sexual sin divides and destroys people.

Sexual sin divides and destroys families.

Sexual sin divides and destroys churches.

And Christ's sacrifice is so life transforming and guilt removing that in repentance of sin, sexual sinners are not destroyed—even if they lose everything they ever loved and worked so hard to attain. Jesus is the true Passover Lamb. He truly delivers us from bondage. When the elders exercised church discipline, we all got to know each other better than we ever wanted to. Things got hard. Fast.

Very few of us in our church knew each other well enough to know our past or present sins until this happened. Suddenly there was no place to hide. Our private worlds were on display.

People turned on each other. Fingers pointed outward.

One camp felt strongly that these men were clearly unsaved—that knowing better means acting better. Christians—real ones—ought not to still be sinners, this camp maintained.

My husband, our pastor, maintained the biblical position—that sin is deceptive and that Christ's own do fall into the deception, delusion, and power of sin. Sadly. Frighteningly. The Bible teaches that what separates a believer from an unbeliever is repentance. Repentance is a gift from God, and only a believer can repent.

Clearly, Christians sin in big ways. The world already knows that. The church needs to wake up to that. Church discipline confronts that. But what does this mean? If a church member is caught in horrific, dangerous sin, does this mean that he is not really saved? These debates divided us.

The Bible reveals that sin is not a matter of knowing better. If it were, we would not need grace through the atoning Savior, Jesus Christ. Sin is deceptive. It takes people captive. Sin is more than a bad idea over which you have complete control. Within the first handful of pages of the Bible, God says to Cain, "Sin is crouching at the door. Its desire is contrary to you, but you must rule over it" (Gen. 4:7). The same is true for us. Sin lurks with the power to deceive. Sin knows where we live. And the only way to rule over it is to watch out for it. We must submit all desires to Christ's authority. The minute that you exalt any desire of yours over Christ's clear command, you are a dead man. Deception means no less than this:

an evil force is out to get you, to own you by the use of your own sinful churnings, and to take you captive to do its will. With the blink of an eye, you become complicit with your captor. You become that which you formerly loathed. Every single thing you ever worked for and valued can disintegrate in your very hands within thirty seconds.

But knowing better should mean something, yes? Yes. It really should. Knowing better should make you watchful over temptation. It should make you fear God. It should snap you out of any delusion you have about having control over your sin. It should make you guard against any teaching that makes any sin seem tolerable, acceptable, and understandable. If you can't hate your sin, you can't fight your sin. Knowing better means something before you fall, as it warns you of serious danger—but after you are snared by your sin, knowing better will not help you. You need Jesus the rescuer to do that. You need the gift and grace of repentance. And church discipline sounds the alarm.

Church discipline is a wake-up call to flee to Christ and to stop trying to hide. But for those who believe that knowing better covers it, church discipline brings out the sin of pride. It makes people say things like, "I could never do that!" It cultivates in folks a longing to be in a church where increasing your social capital means golf and movies, not sackcloth and ashes. These people long for less mess, more intact families. Fewer tattoos, more striped bow ties.

Truly this crisis brought out the Pharisee in us all.

Our church was devastated. We were frail to begin with, having one teaching elder (Kent, our pastor) and two ruling elders. We were at what we thought was bottom—the weakest we could be. Two months after deposing one ruling elder for unrepentant sin, we lost the other to exhaustion and ill-health. Our presbytery supplied provisional elders, good men, but men who lived in Indiana. With no local elders and a church bleeding out at a major artery, Kent's work now tripled. He was stretched as thin as I have ever seen him. His Fitbit recorded the collateral damage: two and three hours of sleep each night. Our new, dangerous norm.

In spite of exhaustion, Kent doubled down. He was committed to keeping as many ministries in place as possible. We continued hosting Kids Club at our house on Friday nights, playing capture the flag as the fireflies came out, as if our only care in the world was a touchdown and a snatched red bandana and the laughter of children. We were desperate to find our balance, hoping that as we flew like the wind over the makeshift finish line, we would arrive somewhere safe. We longed for solid ground.

Kent's stress cough came back. He needed all the help he could get.

Instead of help, he got something else.

Three large families in unison took aim at both the sinners and the church elder board (called a "session" in Presbyterian churches). Formerly strong and steady and set apart as our future leaders, these families flipped from being stakeholders and supporters to becoming our vocal critics. They found fault with the very things they once praised our little church for—from the preaching to the community fellowship.

They sought greener pastures. They did not want to be in a church that had to bear the grief of church discipline, with all of its unanswered questions and with the slow and faltering process of pleading and praying for repentance. They wanted more for their children—more fun, more joy in the Lord, more church growth, more proof that we Christians are on the winning team, more children to have more fun with. Who could blame them? Nothing like unrepentant sin in response to church discipline reveals the pitiful reality that, truly, we are mere men.

Our dire situation pointed to this: we stand in the risen Christ alone, or we do not stand at all.

When we lost the big families, at first everything seemed hollow. The congregational singing was weak. The children's program went from three large age-organized classes to one class for everyone. I went back to teaching children's Sunday school and to taking my rotation in leading congregational singing. Kent now was the only available teacher for the adult Sunday school program, the only preacher, and the only counselor on site.

The shock of seeing the decamping of what we feebly thought were the church's future leaders was devastating. It felt like we were living with an amputation. In the grief of loss, we learned how to pray as a body in ways we hadn't done before.

Like most pastors' wives who are also mothers, I felt an immediate pain for my husband and my children in the loss of these big families. We loved those families and those children. We missed them.

The few tiny families and single covenant households that stayed were humbled by the work ahead, by the devastation in our midst, and by the reality that Christ can use anything that humbles us to glorify himself and raise us—and our church—from the dead. Dealing with sin is not for the faint of heart. We are weak people. We felt the call of lamentation. It was like being at a never-ending funeral.

During the two years that these discipline cases were going on, even as long shadows seemed cast on the First Reformed Presbyterian Church of Durham, we continued to practice daily, messy, open hospitality. Kent continued to preach faithfully and lead Sunday school and a Wednesday night Bible study/prayer meeting. And our church continued to receive visitors and even new members. People started to visit and then stayed. Many came from churches that eschewed church discipline. They saw in our church faithful preaching and sacrificial Christian living. All I saw was a disaster. In spite of my sadness and sin, the church grew.

One of my greatest worries during this time was the spiritual well-being of Knox and Mary. They had not made professions of faith. My concern was that if all they saw was the hard and the heavy, they never would.

Also during this time, the provisional elders set a boundary for our home hospitality. The deposed and excommunicated elder did not have open access to our open hospitality. He was not allowed in—not until the elders gave the green light. Our unrepenting former elder seemingly didn't understand what repentance required of him. The provisional elders stepped in, not only to counsel him and his family, but to protect our home hospitality.

———

And all this raises a question: do church discipline and Christian hospitality cancel each other out? This point might seem esoteric, as too few churches actually practice either radically ordinary hospitality or faithful church discipline. But Christian churches are called to practice both. And we practice both. And therefore this question has to be asked. Are people under church discipline allowed to participate in open table fellowship? There isn't a pat answer. Each situation is different. The elders make this call.

The boundaries that surround table fellowship and home hospitality during public church-discipline cases will be different in different cases, as the elders know the situation better than the membership—perhaps even better than immediate family members. They will know if church members under discipline are potentially dangerous to the body. Good elders set boundaries without disclosing confidences.

But make no mistake: it is a million times safer to include unbelieving neighbors and people who have not claimed the blood of Christ or the citizenship of the church than to let a potential Judas run loose in the church.

Atheists do far less harm than hypocrites.

What Is Church Discipline?

To become a covenant member of my church, I took seven membership vows. One of the vows deals with church discipline, and, for me, it was the vow that gave me considerable anxiety. It is a long vow, and its last line reads this way: "In case you should need correction in doctrine or life, do you promise to respect the authority and discipline of the church?" The vow makes a simple point—discipline is central to discipleship, and every member of a church is a stakeholder.

In my eighteen years in this denomination, I have witnessed four discipline cases. Each case involved a public sin, which necessitated a public announcement. And in each tender, wretched situation, the pastor announced the case in tears, with the humility that knows we are all capable of all sin.

Church discipline has one main purpose: to reconcile the sinning brother or sister to God and to the people sinned against, through repentance and a change of heart and conduct. This one main purpose also has five additional outcomes: (1) to wake up a member of the church to the serious danger he or she is in; (2) to issue a serious warning to others in the body about the danger of the particular sin; (3) to maintain the purity of Christ's church and unity and peace within the body; (4) to uphold the truth of the gospel; and (5) to avoid God's wrath coming upon the church. Discipline in the household of faith shows that whom God loves, he chastises. There is no greater folly than toying with the things of God.

Church discipline is soul preserving. Biblical church discipline has five incremental levels: (1) admonition (used in a neglect of duty, and even for more serious sins); (2) rebuke (used for continued lack of duty); (3) suspension of privileges of membership, including participation in the Lord's Supper (used for gross sin or persistent neglect); (4) deposition, or removing an ordained officer from his office (used for gross sin on the part of a church officer); (5) excommunication (for unrepentant sin; this means exclusion from the visible church).

From a certain perspective, this might seem invasive. It might seem infantilizing to have someone—even your pastor and your elders—tell you what you can and cannot do. Godly church discipline depends on proper oversight from and accountability to elders who, in love, seek to reclaim a lost sheep. Church discipline appeals to the heart of a brother (or sister) who has grown deaf to God's warning, to draw him back, to restore him. Having a teachable spirit means inviting correction.

From another perspective, church discipline might seem too intimate. How in the world does your pastor know you well enough to anticipate when you might stumble? God works through the pastor and the elders in a special way. The pastor must be in the lives of his people. But how is this possible?

Our church is used to regular, scheduled home visits, where pastors and elders are customarily in the homes of each member, learning about the particular struggles and gifts that each person and family has. Those in this family of God are known to one another. Our struggles are not hidden—or, at least, they ought not to be.

Bible-believing Christians know that sin renders some people into victims. In each of the church discipline cases I have witnessed, there are victims. The victims in these cases have all been women. People who have been victimized by members of a church need to be restored as well. Books such as *Restoring the Soul of a Church* can aid the church in restoring and serving those who have been wounded.[1] Victims of sexual misconduct must be taken seriously. They must have their accusations fairly investigated, and if the accusations are substantiated, the victims must be supported and believed. They must be reminded that the sin was not their fault. They must know that the church will not allow the perpetrator to have access to other potential victims. They must hear an apology from the perpetrator and perhaps from the church. This is all very painful business.

According to the *New Dictionary of Biblical Theology*, the purpose of church discipline at every level is to bring about repentance. But how does this work? How does discipline bring forth repentance? How is church discipline, biblically defined, hospitable? How is church discipline a lifeboat in tempestuous waters?

I believe that church discipline is God's kindness; it is God's protection to each church member. It stops perpetrators, and it heals victims. Repentance changes everything. And the Bible records the call to repentance as a signature kindness given by the Holy Spirit: "Do you presume on the riches of his kindness and forbearance and patience, not knowing that God's kindness is meant to lead you to repentance?" (Rom. 2:4). I have known too many people who wake up to a toxic sin problem in their life only after it has exploded and destroyed everything they have ever loved and touched. Church discipline seeks to wake up brothers and sisters before sin's consequences take over. And while it is never too late to repent—where there is life, there is hope—it is often too late to repair circumstances. Church discipline seeks to help members exercise the spiritual disciplines and make the necessary changes before that happens.

If a member is under church discipline, he or she receives counsel and discipleship from the pastor and elders, with the end goal of seeing the fruit of repentance. This brother or sister receives a great deal of attention. In a small church, the one under discipline sucks up resources of time, energy, and everything else that the pastor and elders have to give. It is hard and painful work. The provisional elders appointed to help us have flown and driven down to North Carolina from Indiana to aid us in times of need. As a pastor's wife, I have seen the gritty, behind-the-scenes sadness of the process, as I have watched my husband faithfully pray, counsel, and plead. There are times when it seems that the most high-maintenance people in the church suck up all the resources and then turn on their heels and leave.

During this season of intense counseling and persuading, it is important that the one under discipline not be the subject of gossip or the perpetrator of it. Especially in the case of grievous sin with multiple and present victims, it is paramount that table fellowship in the home not become the occasion to interfere with the process of church discipline. Satan would love nothing more than to use your good intentions to further his destruction. In truth, your pastor and elders have more information than you do. Pray for your elders and pray for the member under church discipline, and if you have information that the elders don't have, by all means tell them. But don't think you know more than you actually do.

First Corinthians 5 contains the classic biblical text dealing with church discipline:

> It is actually reported that there is sexual immorality among you, and of a kind that is not tolerated even among pagans, for a man has his father's wife. And you are arrogant! Ought you not rather to mourn? Let him who has done this be removed from among you. (vv. 1–2)

In that passage Paul was confronting the sin of incest. To compound the problem, the congregation in Corinth was complicit—church members congratulated themselves for their open-mindedness. In today's church parlance, we would call it a "welcoming congregation." Matthew 18:15–20 guides us in how to respond to someone who sins against us: before involving the whole church, we go privately to the offender. If private confrontation does not bring about repentance and reconciliation, then the church is to be brought in. In Corinth the apostle Paul was dealing with a sinful situation in which he had no personal involvement, yet the impact of the sin was felt church-wide. Public sins, including heresy or bad teaching, must be dealt with publicly, because public sins cast a wide net in encouraging others to sin. Anything less than public repentance of a public sin abnegates a believer's responsibility before God and church. Paul told the church to purge the sin and the sinner in order to bring him to repentance. This is tough love, to be sure.

Paul here is recommending church discipline. And in order to wake up the man committing incest, Paul also needs to deal with the congregation. He tells the congregation, "Your boasting is not good" (1 Cor. 5:6). He also spells out the boundaries of this church discipline: "I am writing to you not to associate with anyone who bears the name of brother if he is guilty of sexual immorality or greed, or is an idolater, reviler, drunkard, or swindler—not even to eat with such a one" (1 Cor. 5:11). Paul is distinguishing the church member who sins sexually (the "brother") from outsiders, who are not under the oversight of the church, but instead will be judged by God. Paul writes: "Is it not those inside the church whom you are to judge? God judges those outside. Purge the evil person from among you" (1 Cor. 5:12–13). That is strong, decisive language. Paul does not seek to understand the man's motives for committing incest. Paul doesn't ask the man to explain his thinking. The man committing incest must be removed. The congregation must be made to stop its complicity. This is a wake-up call. Paul is sounding the alarm, for the sake of their souls and for the integrity of the church.

In my Bible I have Rex and Ben's names written in the margins by 2 Corinthians 2:7–8: "You should . . . turn to forgive and comfort him, or he may be overwhelmed by excessive sorrow. So I beg you to reaffirm your love for him." In the church in Corinth, the man in an incestuous relationship with his stepmother stopped and repented and was restored back into the church. We long for a similar outcome. I wrote Rex and Ben's names in my Bible when Kent was preaching through this passage, and I felt personally convicted of my sin of hating them. For hate them, I did.

Kent was preaching to a very small group that day, as the mass exodus of families left only fifteen members. But the conviction of sin I felt from the Lord through Kent's preaching was thundering.

As a congregation we have seen conviction of sin followed by repentance in one church-disciplined man. Paul's call—to "turn to forgive and comfort him, or he may be overwhelmed by excessive sorrow. So I beg you to reaffirm your love for him"—is weighty. It is the moment that Paul had been desiring all along, that the man who had committed a heinous crime would come back and publicly repent. And in this passage Paul calls the congregation to rally around the repentant sinner. Paul wants the congregation to be complicit—not with sin, but with repentance. Repentance is the threshold to God. My conviction of sin made me realize that I cannot protect myself from sin—mine or someone else's. Only God can.

Repentance gives glory to God. Kent reminded the congregation of this general biblical principle over and over again as we waded through the grief and shame. Kent continued to bring us back to Joshua 7:19:

> Joshua said to Achan, "My son, give glory to the LORD God of Israel and give praise to him. And tell me now what you have done; do not hide it from me."

Joshua's plea followed a shameful military defeat, after which the Lord revealed to Joshua that sin in the camp had caused it. After examining the camp, the sin was revealed to be Achan's. He stole from among the spoil, and then he buried his ill-gotten treasure in the ground. His eyes wandered. He coveted. He stole. He hid. His sin caused defeat, discouragement, and death. This is where most commentators go with Achan. But that was not where Kent was going.

Kent wanted us to see that repentance bears fruit, and even if we must pay the price for the sin, when we repent, we give God glory. Repentance always bears the fruit of giving glory to God. Repentance is not an end point; it is a launching pad. We repent unto holiness. In repentance we grow in Christlikeness. We show that God is always right about matters of sin and grace. Our soul is refreshed and made ready to die well, even if, like Achan, die we must. So repentance refreshes the believer, gives glory to God, and bears Christian fruit. Repentance is a gift from God, for only believers can repent.

And back in 1 Corinthians 5, a public sinner's repentance makes Paul overjoyed. Paul knows how deep real repentance goes—how it undoes a sinner and remakes him, and how it leaves him raw, vulnerable, and transparent. I imagine Paul—years after the Lord had made him an apostle, years after his days of slaughtering Christians for religious zeal—breaking bread with a fellow believer and recognizing something in the shape of an eye, the turning up of a nose, the tone of a laugh or cry. I also imagine the horror that could have seized him, stopped him, made him gasp for breath. I can feel the recognition: that eye, that nose, that voice, so similar to someone he had murdered. Paul may have found himself at table fellowship with the children of a faithful mother he had killed in his pharisaical zeal.

Repentance changes everything. Through it, you become something you could never imagine. And repentance is a gift from God. It cannot be manufactured or faked.

Lost Sheep and Prowling Wolves

What if we are dealing not with a lost sheep but instead with a wolf in the church?

There is a book that has stayed open and on my desk for years now. It is *The Suffering Saviour: A Series of Devotional Meditations* by the German Reformed pastor F. W. Krummacher, first published in 1856. It is a powerful book and a daily reminder of who Jesus is and what he really does. And who we are, apart from him.

Krummacher's chapter on Judas Iscariot is especially arresting, and I have read and reread it many times. He writes something about Judas that the church needs to confront. He says: "The heathen world has no Judas, and could not produce such a character. Such a monster matures only in the radiant sphere of Christianity. He entered into too close contact with the Savior not to become entirely His or wholly Satan's."[2] Krummacher was making the point that one should never toy with the things of God. In other words, you should never boast about a relationship with Jesus that is based on what you hope to get out of it. Dare never to get close to Jesus just for the public appearance. Never confuse knowing facts with knowing the Shepherd. It's all or nothing. Either Jesus owns your heart, or you are exalting yourself to your immanent destruction.

Words like Krummacher's crawl up my spine. "He entered into too close contact with the Savior not to become entirely His or wholly Satan's."

The scene where the heart of Judas is revealed takes place at the home of Simon the leper in the context of hospitality and table fellowship. In both life and Scripture, Christian hospitality is the place where truth is often revealed and people are exposed. And truth is edgy. Truth is divisive. Jesus died for the truth. Are we willing to live for it?

As we consider this hard fact from 1 Corinthians 5—that the church often facilitates and covers the sins of its Judases—let's keep in mind two other passages of Scripture:

> Now when Jesus was at Bethany in the house of Simon the leper, a woman came up to him with an alabaster flask of very expensive ointment, and she poured it on his head as he reclined at table. And when the disciples saw it, they were indignant, saying, "Why this waste? For this could have been sold for a large sum and given to the poor." But Jesus, aware of this, said to them, "Why do you trouble the woman? For she has done a beautiful thing to me." (Matt. 26:6–10)

> But Judas Iscariot, one of his disciples (he who was about to betray him), said, "Why was this ointment not sold for three hundred denarii and given to the poor?" He said this, not because he cared about the poor, but because he was a thief, and having charge of the moneybag he used to help himself to what was put into it. Jesus said, "Leave her alone, so that she may keep it for the day of my burial. For the poor you always have with you, but you do not always have me." (John 12:4–8)

Let's first look at the characters in Matthew 26:6–10, as they provide a literary landscape for us to see ourselves.

Simon the Leper

Why is Simon known as "Simon the leper"? Who was he, and why was he known for his leprosy? He clearly wasn't still a leper at this time. Why is he still remembered as such? Of this passage Matthew Henry writes:

> Probably, he was one who had been miraculously cleansed from his leprosy by our Lord Jesus, and he would express his

gratitude to Christ . . . to come in to him, and sup with him. Though he was cleansed, yet he was called *Simon the leper*. Those who are guilty of scandalous sins, will find that, though the sin be pardoned, the reproach will cleave to them.[3]

This may be very hard to hear, but it is a truth that must sink in. Sins against which cultures erect taboos—incest, homosexuality, prostitution—are forgiven and put, once and for all, under the blood of Christ for those who turn and repent. The pardoning of sin does not come with the removal of reproach. The Bible records these as sins of a high and mighty order.

Mary

And who is this Mary? Most think she is Mary the sister of Lazarus, who had spent time at the feet of Jesus learning not only from him but also about him. She knew his teaching, and she knew the man-God himself. She knew the oil would provide the physical refreshment and restoration that would lift his spirits. And she knew that Jesus was worth it. The oil symbolizes the gospel message itself: it is both costly and worth it.

But it was very extravagant oil, and she had an "alabaster," or a Roman pound, the monetary equivalent needed to feed bread to eight hundred people.[4] Where in the world did people of modest means get hold of an "alabaster" of this good oil? Edersheim speculates:

> Mary may have had that alabaster of very costly ointment from olden days, before she had learned to serve Christ. Then, when she came to know him, and must have learned how constantly [his death], of which he ever spoke, was before His Mind, she may have put it aside, kept it, against the day of His burying. And now the decisive hour had come.[5]

Mary knew better than the others that Jesus was about to fulfill the Scripture, that his appointed hour to die, save, and rise again was now.

Perhaps this is why Jesus says that "wherever this gospel is proclaimed in the whole world, what she has done will also be told in
memory of her" (Matt 26:13). What had she done? She had listened
to the Lord, and she knew that fulfilling the Scriptures would require his blood. She discerned the times and was not moved by
either sentimentality or wishful thinking; she saw it starkly. His
time had come. And she gave him everything she had—she placed
upon him her heart, her dreams, her hope, and her trust. She did
not know how this would work out, but she knew the Lord, and
knowing who he really was meant that she could anoint his feet,
withstand the criticism of the disciples, and remain steadfast.

And while Mary was giving all to the Lord, walking in faith,
the disciples were complaining about Mary's hospitality. It was
too ostentatious. Too expensive. And, unbeknownst to anyone
but Jesus, it was cramping Judas's style. Judas was helping himself to the money set aside for the poor. He was stealing from God
Almighty. And because he had become practiced—and therefore
hardened—in this sin, his heart was hard, and he felt entitled to
take at will.

The drama here is compelling. As Edersheim notes, the light
of Mary's faith "cast the features of Judas in gigantic dark out-
lines against the scene. He knew the nearness of Christ's betrayal,
and hated the more; she knew the nearness of [Christ's] precious
death, and loved the more."[6]

The world can produce evil dictators, but only the church can
grow a Judas. Dictators intend to control; they start as hypocrites.
Not so Judases. Krummacher writes:

> At the moment when he offered his services, he was no hyp-
> ocrite, at least not consciously so. And when he afterward
> prayed, studied the Word of God, and even preached it with
> the other disciples, it was doubtless done for a time with a
> degree of inward truthfulness. [But] amid pious sentiment, an
> evil root remained within, which was the love of the world.[7]

How could something as commonplace as the love of the world

turn a disciple into a monster? It happened slowly, step by step, getting close enough to Jesus to feel intrigued by his teaching but never being broken by it, never really knowing the God-man Shepherd, never dying to self and being remade by his soon-to-be-cross-punctured hands.

Jesus offered a mild rebuke to Judas when he said, "Why do you trouble the woman? For she has done a beautiful thing to me" (Matt. 26:10). And the words of Jesus landed on a hard heart, so hard that entitlement to that which was only his in the delusion of pride bubbled up. Judas responded to Jesus in self-righteous anger. In his heart and in his actions, he said, "You have no rights to me, not to this deep and private part of me. I will have what I want." Judas was saying in his actions, "You, Jesus, failed me. You did not give me what I prayed for." He missed the core lesson: a heart broken by Jesus asks the Lord to make him godly, not bless his natural desires. A heart broken by Jesus prays, "Lord, make me yours," not, "Lord, give me what I want."

Krummacher says, "The light of the world was to him a burning fire; the savior of sinners. . . . [Christ was] an inquisitor before whom he must either expose himself as a guilty criminal, or envelop himself in the veil of hypocritical deceit; and he chose the latter."[8] He chose. In his heart, he chose.

But things didn't go south for Judas at such lightning speed that he could be rendered an innocent victim. On the outside, things looked okay. But then there was table fellowship, that dinner party with Mary and the precious oil, and Judas lost it. With cocksure pride he publicly rebuked Mary—and I suspect he was confident all would agree with him, for that is how blind sin makes a man. In response, the Lord issued a rebuke as gentle as the Savior himself. This was church discipline in the making. And in response, Judas flared seething rage deep inside. This is always a deadly combination—a gentle rebuke from Jesus and a flaring rage of entitlement by an image bearer in response. Ironically, this heart sin asks a vital question: *Who are you to treat me this way?* But it doesn't stay quiet long enough to hear the Lord's answer.

What slowed down this scene, giving Judas time that he could have used differently? Table fellowship. It gives people the time and place to confess. What would Judas do?

> The erring disciple must now either cast himself down at Jesus' feet, with streams of penitential tears and seek, by a frank confession of his lost condition, deliverance, and mercy at the throne of grace; or his mortified pride must gain the victory, and by urging him to the opposite course of a willful hardening, afford Satan the opportunity of imparting the infernal spark of secret bitterness against [Jesus].[9]

Is It I, Lord?

But there was even more going on there. There were disciples there who asked the right question. There were onlookers for whom church discipline cast a powerful warning, a lesson learned, a life that would stay the course.

> And as they were eating, [Jesus] said, "Truly, I say to you, one of you will betray me." And they were very sorrowful and began to say to him one after another, "Is it I, Lord?" He answered, "He who has dipped his hand in the dish with me will betray me. The Son of Man goes as it is written of him, but woe to that man by whom the Son of Man is betrayed! It would have been better for that man if he had not been born." (Matt. 26:21–24)

The humility of the eleven faithful ought not be overlooked. "Is it I?" is the best question that any disciple can ever ask when Jesus warns about sin, when any church discipline takes place, whenever we hear about the sin committed by someone else. As we turn the pages of our hearts over against the pages of the Bible each morning, we ought to ask, "Is it I?" These three words reveal the heart of true believers, who know that they are capable of any imaginable sin and that it is only Christ's saving grace indwelling them that reveals the truth about them and their desires. "Is it I?" are the assembled words by which the believer discovers himself— the condemning nature of his sin, the recreation of self in Christ.

And what if you ask that question, and the Lord says, "Yes, it is you." Then what? Well, then, you must fall on your face and repent of your sin. There are two ways to ask the question, "Is it I?" One way is with a teachable heart, one that is willing to repent when the Lord exposes sin. The other is with a hard heart, using the question as a way to demand that the Lord become your debate partner, that he explain on your terms why your sin is so very intolerable. And when Judas ate the bread that marked him as traitor, "the day of salvation closed; the hour of the visitation or divine mercy expired; the angels of peace sorrowfully removed from his side, and Satan triumphantly entered into him."[10]

The lesson here is a terrible one, truly, for Judases are everywhere. Without intending it, many churches have cultivated the making of a Judas. They have lost their way. They think themselves more merciful than God. They think the Bible is too severe, asks too much of people. They produce Judases in their seminaries, they place them in their pulpits, and they replicate them in their pews. The lesson is this: "Neutrality is a forlorn position. He that enters but half-way into the prevailing tendency of the present day, finishes his course before he is aware that he is in the snare of the devil."[11]

As we gather around my table, a church family wounded by sin, protected by church discipline, renewed by the repentance of a restored brother, we cannot help but ask, "Is it I, Lord?" All the faithful must ask, "Is it I, Lord? I am capable of betraying you. I am weak, but you are strong. Keep me. Preserve me." As David pens for us: "Preserve me, O God, for in you I take refuge. / I say to the LORD, 'You are my Lord; / I have no good apart from you'" (Ps. 16:1–2). The presence of Judas in the church sets boundaries of care and protection and kindness around hospitality. We are better for this. As Peter commands, "Therefore, brothers, be all the more diligent to confirm your calling and election, for if you practice these qualities you will never fall" (2 Pet. 1:10). When we proclaim the gospel to one another, which we must do, even as Christ followers, we help each other ask, "Is it I, Lord? Am I your betrayer?" We do this to work repentance deep in our hearts. We want grace, but we know that we cannot bypass repentance to get God's grace. We all can be deceived. Asking this question of ourselves and others is a kindness, not a condemnation.

———

And what about our little church?

The Lord saw us through that hard time. He grew us in grace and in numbers. People hungry for God's grace and truth started coming and staying and making a covenant of church membership and building distinct ministries to the outsiders and the outcasts. Children started coming too. And during the rubble of difficulty and hardship, Knox and Mary committed their lives to Jesus. By God's grace. By grace alone, not because church is fun or big or because all their friends are here. No, not at all. Only because Jesus is who he says he is.

7

Giving up the Ghosts

The Lamentation of Hospitality

February 3, 2017, Durham, North Carolina

This morning, when my alarm chirped at four o'clock, I intuitively reached for a sweater of my mom's that still smells of her. The sweater smells like jasmine and Suave hair spray and tea tree oil.

My mother and I were too close and not close at all. I was her only child, and for most of my life, I suffocated under her dashed expectations.

My mother was an early feminist who raised a feminist daughter. When I was about five years old, I recall being in the elevator of Marshall Fields in Chicago. A (somewhat creepy, as I remember him) man bent down, got too close to my face, smelling sickeningly of Old Spice (too sweet!) and Brandywine pipe tobacco (too stale!), and breathed, "What a pretty little girl. Are you going to marry a doctor?" My mother, who stood 4 feet 11 inches high, wedged herself between me and this man and declared, "My daughter is not going to *marry* a doctor. She is going to *become* one." From that day forward, my fate was set, and the churning of women's empowerment and independence from men became my driving idols.

My mother was also manic, and until she admitted this to a doctor in 2008—at the age of seventy-seven—and started taking medication to control it, she was unbearable to be around. No majestic mountain range knew the heights of her excitement, and no cavernous depth knew the pit of her anger and despair. My job was to keep jollying her out of mental illness to stay somewhere in the middle. I spent my life trying to orchestrate my mother's mental health, and I failed miserably.

For most of our years together, it was just she and I. My half-brother disappeared from my life when I turned ten; my father was absent through alcohol abuse and a secret life of white-collar petty crime long before he passed away, seven days after my twenty-second birthday.

My mother was fundamentally unable to keep friends over the long haul, when her unpredictable anger canceled out her effusive giving, but my mom was able to make friends in the snap of a smile. Mom was personable, funny, gregarious, and the life of the party.

When I was a new professor at Syracuse University, my lover at the time, Kate, would bring me home to her father and stepmother's house. They lived a few miles from our home. Together with Bill and Janet (Kate's dad and stepmom), we would play bridge and drink merlot, go bowling and then out for Mexican food, take in the festival at Sylvan Beach and play dopey carnival games. We would stay up in our pj's and watch movies together. When we stayed at their house, Kate and I could spend hours working on our books or go for a long run. We could come to their home when it was convenient and leave when we needed to. We were not shamed for our absence or criticized for our presence. I'd never before known that you could actually relax in the presence of parents. After my first weekend with them, I was overcome with grief and sadness for all the "what might have beens" in my relationship with my parents.

By contrast, in the presence of my mother, my job was to anticipate her every emotional need, body block all conversations that disobeyed her lordship, and, using any means available, keep her from exploding. But I failed. If explosion and implosion were "love languages," then these were my mother's only two.

Once I came out as a lesbian, Kate and others in my lesbian community rightly diagnosed my relationship with my mother as "toxic" and "codependent." (There are no two stronger words of condemnation in the lesbian community, so I knew to take this seriously.) I started to put more distance between my mom and me—which meant instead of talking with her multiple times each day, I tried to talk with her once a week. She didn't take this lightly, but I seized the opportunity of my mother's remarriage and relocation to Scottsdale, Arizona, as my ticket to escape.

Mom married Theo when I was in graduate school, and he was a wonderful influence and distraction. But my mom did not like boundaries between us, and she still found reasons to call me every day. I bristled under the tight leash. But with her new marriage, my mother's class elevated. I cherished the European vacations my mother and her new husband took, as phone calls were cost prohibitive during those seasons. It was wonderful to breathe.

My mother took my lesbianism in stride. It wasn't her first choice for me, but she was wary of men. A sexual-abuse survivor, my mom had no illusions. As long as I kept my focus on tenure and success, she could respect my choices.

Then I came out as a Christian, and all hell broke loose.

Theo was a bridge. He was calm and funny and smart. He was at ease in all social settings. He loved good books. He read *The New York Times* cover to cover daily; he read the entire book review section each week (as I do). He handled all the crazy changes in my life like the Renaissance man that he was. So when I came out as a Christian, he took that in stride too. He had graduated from seminary, following in the footsteps of his father, who was a Greek Orthodox priest. But in seminary, Theo came to believe that the New Testament was untrue, untenable, untrustworthy, and indefensible. He left his faith for PhD work at the University of Chicago and the Massachusetts Institute of Technology (MIT), and went on to become a self-made millionaire before turning fifty.

Theo was unflappable. When I became a Christian, Theo became my Greek tutor. Teaching me Greek was one of our many connections. (I didn't get much past the alphabet, but our relationship went deeper than my language acquisition through this tutoring.)

When my mom started to take medication for her mental illness in 2008, Theo started to show signs of dementia. It was a mild and sweet dementia though, and they decided to move to Virginia to spend Theo's last years with our children, whom he loved. The grandchildren called him "Papoo"—Greek for "Grandpa"—and after a while, we all called him "Papoo." Our years together in Virginia were sweet. Zoloft meant Mom was functional for the first time in her life, and without the fugue of mania, her gifts of hospitality and caregiving shone with luster. She tied in to our homeschooling, to our neighboring, and to our children's swimming lessons and bird walks and homeschool coop.

Mom retreated, though, when anything connected to the church came to the forefront or when Kent's sister and brother-in-law came to town. She was insanely jealous of both, of the way that both the body of Christ and Kent's family loved us and loved us well. If she couldn't win at something, she wouldn't play at all.

My mother demanded idolatrous obedience. As Theo was dying, he was growing to love the things of God. Even in dementia, Papoo looked forward to family devotions and would ask me to sing psalms to him after dinner, after the dishes were wiped, the dogs walked, and the children in bed. Once as we were clearing dishes, my mom rebuked Theo: "I thought we agreed that the Christian religion was crap!"

"Maybe I'm changing my mind, Dee," he replied softly.

In 2011, at the age of eighty-nine, Papoo was dying at home with hospice. My mom was a tireless caregiver during his death days. We kept baby monitors in his room so we could hear him when we weren't at his bedside. Mom was vigilant. One day my mom and I were having coffee in the kitchen, and we could hear the children talking with Papoo over the baby monitor. Mary was singing Psalm 23, and then she started talking. Mary, age five at the time, had a speech impediment that turned words upside down and all around. (We later learned that this is an indicator of dyslexia.) My mom hushed me so she could hear. As Mary's sweet, mangled words came into clarity, my mother was growing more and more furious. Mary was sharing the gospel with a piercing clarity that no speech impediment could abate.

"Papoo, where you go when die? Jesus be with you? Christian? Jesus Shepherd?"

Papoo understood every word she said. He answered her like this: "Little Mary, I am a Christian. I have made peace with Jesus, my Shepherd. At long last. I love you."

Mary, thrilled, came running into the kitchen. "Hear you did? Hear you did?" she squealed in her backward-word language. My mother cursed, threw the book she held in her hand across the room, and stomped out of the apartment.

Papoo passed away on August 11, 2011.

One year later, Kent received a call to pastor the First Reformed Presbyterian Church in Durham, North Carolina. We all thought it would be best if Mom moved with us. I really don't know why we thought this. Perhaps we didn't want to leave her in Virginia after she had just moved there to be with us. Perhaps we were lured by the thought of buying a nice house together after years of being house-poor in the outer DC suburbs. I still have a hard time motive-checking this decision. Why had I put so much faith in my mother's Zoloft as to live in the same house with her again, something I had sworn I would never, ever do? Idols are funny monsters, and they spring up like shape-shifting weeds, promising that things will be different this time.

My mother lived with our family for sixteen months, from April of 2012 until October of 2013, when she moved from our home to a retirement home two miles away. The elders wanted Kent to be installed at First Reformed Presbyterian Church of

Durham right away. Mom put up the down payment for our house in Durham. My mother was exceedingly generous, but her generosity came with strings. I was grateful when our house in Northern Virginia sold a month after we moved and we could pay her back. But the ties that bind transcended debt paid. It was then that I noticed it: only when Jesus pays the debt is it truly paid in full.

Living with her was miserable, and I am sure she would say the same thing about living with us. I hated myself for having put my family through it. The hard edges of my childhood, which had receded into a gentle place of memory with distance and wishful thinking, came back with full force. My mother was angry, controlling, shaming of my children, undermining of my husband, and condemning of our faith. Family devotions became a battleground. And Kent was trying to be the new pastor of a church that was busting at the seam with decade-long sin that was just now creeping out of the foundation.

Those were spiritually rich days, as bitter desperation leaves only gospel promises sweet. These days forced me to deal in Christian love with daily battles. My mother was unhappy from the minute she woke up until the minute she went to bed. She was critical of the house we bought together, the people she lived with (including her grandchildren, whom she loved more than anything), and anything else that came to mind. She stopped taking her medication (Zoloft)—cold turkey. She would rage unpredictably. She would buy so many paper products from Amazon Prime Pantry that we could not store them or fit the cardboard boxes in the recycling bin. We were afraid to do hospitality of any sort. I felt miserable that I was subjecting my family to reruns of my humiliating childhood. I felt guilty that I was prohibiting my husband from doing the ground-zero activity—practicing hospitality—required of pastors. And during these days, the Lord revealed more sin in my heart than I thought any human being could have. I thought that my mother had changed because of Zoloft. I had made Zoloft my idol, my mother's savior, and I had falsely convinced myself that my atheist mother could live in our Christian home because of it.

Kent and I went from being people who were known for hospitality to those whose house was barricaded. We held meetings and dinner parties at the church or at the Eno River State Park. Our home became my familiar prison of horrors. We were daily dreading what my mother might say or do. If you think I am kidding, then read on. I once during this time tried to do a book interview at home. Mary was sick, and I did not want to take her out of the house to go to the church, where I typically conduct interviews in Kent's office. I barricaded myself in my bedroom, gave everyone strict orders not to knock on the door, and put up big signs with bold print marker and construction paper: "Interview in progress. Do not disturb." During this interview, I (and presumably my good Christian host) could hear my mother pounding and screaming at the door, "Sar! Get off that damn phone now! Your damn dog just crapped on the floor, and you need to clean it up now!"

Menopause racked my body, the small church Kent felt called to pastor belched up secret sins deep from both the membership and the elder body, my children grieved the loss of their friends back home and the terror of my mother's screaming, and we were unable to afford the house we had bought. During those years, Kent and I really learned to pray together and have family devotions like we were doing so in a prison cell, and to look with faith at God's promises instead of living in the fear of our circumstances. We prayed for my mother's conversion in a way that we never would have if she had not been living with us. God allowed us to see in these depths how painful it is to live without Christ, how frightening, how hopeless, and how the fruit of the Spirit must be (and can be) exercised in extreme conditions.

When my mom moved out of our home and into a local retirement center two miles away, we all could breathe again. I talked with her daily and had lunch with her weekly, and we as a family gathered together for meals many times per month. But Zoloft wasn't doing the old trick anymore—even when she was taking it as prescribed—and our daily phone calls were just like the old days: a barrage of anger directed against me. Only now, my mother had two more punching bags: Jesus, my Shepherd; and Kent, my husband. That my mother hadn't raised me to be a submitted Christian wife was unequivocal, but here we were, back in the same old place, with my mother's anger and disappointment wrapping itself around me like a noose.

On Christmas Day 2015, my mom had news. She shared it with Kent first. That nagging cough was lung cancer, and she was dying. She wanted to die her way and wanted us to respect that. As a longstanding member of the Hemlock Society (the right-to-die group), it made her weepy that she didn't live in an age when people had the same dignity as a dog, which can be euthanized on request.

When my mom announced she was dying, the noose tightened. I feared many things about my mother's death. I feared most of all—and all the time—for her soul and her eternal future. My mother wasn't just an unbeliever; she was a tested and true atheist. And her atheism had found confirmation when, a few years earlier, someone in our church sinned against her—Big Time.

When we all moved to North Carolina, we had hopes that we could surround her with Christian love, and we prayed that she would even enjoy coming to church with us on the Lord's Day. At first, she did. She seemed to genuinely like the people, especially the older ones. And then one day, somewhat suddenly, she became surly, hostile, angry, and condemning about the people in our church.

A month later I discovered why. Mom was having a hard time balancing her checkbook, and she asked me for help. My mother was sharp about math and money until her last breath, so this was truly odd. She was fifteen hundred dollars off. That it was such a perfect number was really odd too. But Mom assured me that she could never forget writing out a check for that amount, so we went to the bank to see if we could find one missing. We did, and the missing check revealed the secret about why my mom would never walk into our church again. A longstanding leader of our church had cornered Mom as she made her way to the church bathroom and told her that he desperately needed money. He begged her to never tell Kent or me what he was asking her to do. He asked her for fifteen hundred dollars. And she took out her checkbook and wrote him a check, vowing in her heart never to walk back through the doors of this—or any—church again. Like a stalwart wolf in sheep's clothing, he smiled a charming smile and returned to the sanctuary just in time to receive Communion.

It seemed that nothing we did could protect my mother from danger.

Satan not only knew where we lived and how to break through the weak windows; he had made for himself an office within our walls.

But, selfishly, news of my mother's impending death also made me fear for the monster I might become without her. My mother's daily unleashing of anger in some Jekyll-and-Hyde way stopped my own bubbling rage. The idols of my heart poured out like water. It had been me and my mom for fifty-three years, a tangled, toxic, codependent contort. Prior to my conversion to Christ, my mother's daily criticism and unpredictable unleashing of angry words had been my one-way ticket out of her clutches; after conversion, it became the thing that God used best to keep me on my knees.

After my mother told me she was dying, I cleared my travel schedule, rewrote the homeschool schedule to its minimalist program (math and language arts), and hunkered down with her in her apartment, listening as she talked me through old family photos and new financial papers. We cleared out old clothes, and I convinced her to cancel her Amazon Prime Pantry orders of paper products. (Even so, when my mother died, she left me with a year-long supply of toilet paper and 3-ply Kleenex.)

And then Kent and the kids came down with the flu. Then Kent threw his back out. Then I came down with the flu. And, yes, we had all gotten flu shots. By the time I got sick, Kent and the kids were out of bed but still limping along. And Kent's back ached so much he could hardly bend or lift anything.

Two weeks of fever, pain, and bed rest, with Kent doing everything and the kids doing school on the computer—Learning Ally
for Mary and workbooks and math on the computer for Knox. I
talked to my mom on the phone daily, but I can't remember one
thing we said. My uncle and his wife came to town to say goodbye
to my mom, and I can't remember a thing about that either, except
that Kent was going to pick them up at the airport and called our
friend Will, asking if he could come along to carry the baggage that
Kent could not bear.

After two weeks I dragged myself to the doctor, who told me
that I was on the tail end of the flu (duh), prescribed Advil and
liquids, and said, "I need to tell you something that I am not supposed to say."

She revealed to me that during my mother's last appointment,
my mother had removed me from her emergency contact list. The
doctor told me that my mother was being reckless and dangerous
with her health and that I needed to somehow rectify this. I drove
home in a surprise snowstorm (we get these once or twice each
year in the South). I called my mother. No answer. I called the main
line of the Croasdaile Village retirement center. I was told that my
mother had just called an ambulance.

We live in Durham, North Carolina, which is called the City of
Medicine for a reason. One perk in moving Mom with us was that
the medical care here was better than that in Northern Virginia.
But the challenge was also in the bounty. My mom was taken to
the hospital, but which one? We have three hospitals within a ten-
minute drive. Kent was intent on finding her. He got in the car and
started the search.

As it turns out, Mom was taken to Durham Regional Hospital,
and, providentially, my neighbor Bob worked there. Kent showed
up at Regional when he couldn't find Mom at Duke. Bob is one of
our weekly prayer partners, and he had been praying for Mom's
salvation for years. By the time I showered, donned a face mask,
popped 600 mg of Advil, and walked through the door of her hospital room, Bob was entertaining my mother with groanworthy

puns, creating a masterpiece snowflake with recycled Christmas foil and safety scissors (and if you don't believe me, check out his website[1]), and dispensing "pain killers"—a pill bottle filled with colorful Skittles candy. Mom was holding her sides in laughter. But then I froze. I remembered. Mom did not want me there. I was not supposed to be there. Would she lash out at the sight of me? Should I obey her decision to excise me or barge right in? I was weak from flu and not up for battle.

I didn't know what to do, so I stood at the door and prayed.

And when my mom saw me in the door, her eyes softened, and she welcomed all of us in as if she was hosting a dinner party. My mom was clearly thrilled to see us. I wondered what kind of medication she was on.

We visited and made small talk. When Kent took the kids to the vending machine, I nudged the proverbial elephant in the room: "Mom, why did you remove me from your contact list?" With tears in her eyes she said, "I was mad at you, and I forgot that I did that. But I don't want to die without you." And then, as an afterthought, she said: "I like it here. Bob is funny, and they give me morphine."

I often think about this, about the small links and puzzle pieces that make up God's providential care for us. What if Bob had not been there? What if Kent hadn't been able to find her? What if it had been two weeks earlier, and I was in bed with a 103 temperature, unable to move or stay awake? Or four weeks earlier, with my whole family sick with flu and pain? God's providential hand was lovingly guiding each detail.

After two days in the hospital, the doctors declared Mom terminal, and we started to make provisions for hospice. Mom was moved to Hock Family Pavilion and given a private room, and I moved in with her. Kent took over homeschooling and house chores, and I settled into the chair in Mom's room with my Bible, Psalter, and knitting. Deathbeds are unique and holy places. I recall one of the Puritans saying something about repentance being most sweet prior to the Lord's Supper and the deathbed. But my mom was not—in any stretch of anyone's imagination—a believer.

When my mom lived with us for sixteen months, she mocked family devotions, the reading of God's Word, and the use of Christian homeschool curriculum. She believed that science had disproved faith, and this entitled her to do, as she said, whatever the hell she wanted. My mother believed in abortion rights and human euthanasia. She believed that life worth living must be instrumentally valuable. The nurses gently settled Mom in her hospital bed and explained how to use the morphine button. Annie, the sweet social worker who sported a dyke haircut and red Converse high-tops, gave me a good reading light and a pullout cot. Kent took the kids back to Mom's apartment to get her favorite pillow.

When we were finally alone, Mom turned to me, and I could feel the dread rise up in my heart. "Sar, I'm dying my way, not yours. You need to respect that. I have read your books. If anything was going to make me a Christian, it would have been them. But I am not weak. Like you."

The Marxist theorist Raymond Williams declares that certain words and phrases are not merely words: they are keywords— a lingua franca that can launch a revolution or sink a thousand ships. "I am not weak like you" will be forever my keywords. I am weak. As I heard my mother's dying words, I felt that wall of shame wash over me. And then God's Word had the last word in my heart: in my weakness, Christ is strong (2 Cor. 12:9–10).

There is a lot to do beside the bed of a dying mother.

These were busy days, not listless ones.

I realized after the first ten minutes that this is a Christian art, the practice of deathbed hospitality.

Dying people are fickle about pillows and people, the temperature of the water that flows up from a straw, and the way the shades are drawn.

My mother developed peculiar tastes about visitors and avocados and watermelon.

She did not want to see my oldest son, Michael, and his wife (although she loved them in life), but she did want her friends who supported her elected suicide campaign.

I learned how to administer the right amount of water to dying lips, to apply with the right touch emu oil to cracking skin, to lift her weak frame and adjust her back pillow, to push the morphine button when needed. And then, when one of Mom's friends begged me to "put her out of her misery" by overusing morphine, I learned another important art of deathbed hospitality: putting up the "No visitors" sign and unplugging the phone in her room.

And after the fifth of what would become eight days at the deathbed, I realized something: not everyone can come to Christ in the fullness of life—while the world, the flesh, and the Devil are raging and strong. But anyone led by the Spirit can come to Christ on the deathbed, when the flesh is weak. Anyone. Even my mother. But who will lead the way? Who will proclaim the fullness of Christ in the presence of this weakness? If you are not at the deathbed, you can't offer hospitality. Hospitality always requires hands and heads and hearts, and mess and sacrifice and weakness. Always.

It was not easy, because my mother had denied Christ with venom.

But when my mother said that she was weak, I prayed that God would fill her weakness with salvific strength.

So I started where I always start. Singing.

I sang psalms to my mother as she was dying.

I sang through almost the entire Psalter, stopping to repeat some of her favorites: 23, 100, 141.

Nurses began to ask if we could leave the door open so that other patients could hear this beautiful music.

Sometimes medics and ambulance drivers entered her room, took off hats, and sang the bass and tenor parts.

Annie, the Buddhist nurse, was a beautiful alto, and she liked to sight read.

God puts people everywhere to lend a helping hand.

Kent brought more Psalters so that people who wanted to sing with me could pick one up on the way in.

My ten-year-old daughter auditioned to play hymn tunes on the piano so that the residents could hear them as well.

With my daughter in the foyer and me in the rooms of the dying, music of faith became faith's strengthening tonic.

"The Lord is my shepherd, lack nothing shall I. / In lush, verdant pastures, He there makes me lie."[2]

Mom stopped me. She commented, "Having time with you like this, having all of my needs met, this really is a lush and verdant pasture. Dying isn't so bad, as long as I have plenty of morphine."

I kept singing.

"Beside tranquil waters, He leads me along. / Because He restores me, my soul is made strong."[3]

Mom put up her hand and gestured for me to stop and come close.

"I'm dying. I'm becoming weak, not strong. How is my soul being made strong?"

And that is how my world changed in the most powerful gestalt that I have ever experienced, making my own conversion seem sort of pale and soft around the edges.

"Mom, your soul bears God's image, and it will last forever, even as your body wastes away," I whisper. My hands are shaking, and I can barely get the words out.

"You really believe this crap?" utters my mom.

"With all of my heart," I whisper.

"Maybe I am becoming weak like you," Mom muses. "If I'm getting to be soft like you, why don't I understand?" she thinks out loud.

"Mom, I think you understand the gospel. But because you don't know the Shepherd, it seems like nonsense to you," I offer.

"Maybe you're right. So tell me about him. Tell me about the Shepherd. But keep singing, please."

So I sing the rest of Psalm 23:

For His name He leads me on paths that are right,
though I walk the valley where death hides the light.
Since You are there with me, no evil I fear,
Your rod and Your staff give me comfort and cheer.

You set me a table in front of my foes.
My head You anoint and my cup overflows.
Your goodness and love will pursue me each day,
And I in the Lord's house forever will stay.[4]

Something changed in the heavens. In the secret council of the Trinity, one more lost sheep was gathered into the protective arms of her Savior. The stars became brighter. The cosmos shifted. My mom opened her eyes with clarity and said, "Well, that settles it then. I am now weak. I am weak like you. I do need the Shepherd. Now what?"

"Would you like to hear about how to make peace with Jesus?"

"Yes, but first I want to know what I need to do with my sin. And please don't call in a priest."

And with that, everything changed, on earth and in heaven.

My mother wanted me to sing the psalms until I could sing no more.

She wanted Kent to read the Bible and pray and answer all of her questions.

My mother, the former atheist, put her faith in Jesus, repented of her sin, and made peace with God two days before she died.

God is so merciful to me, a sinner.

———

Following are the verses that grounded us together in Christ those last eight days:

Let steadfastness have its full effect, that you may be perfect and complete, lacking in nothing. (James 1:4)

Salvation means that Mom lacks in nothing, that she endured an intense battle with lung cancer, and she placed all her hope in Jesus because there was nothing else left. Indeed, certain experiences are true reflections of the reality of things, and death is one of those. Because of the fall, death is both inevitable and a violent attack against what was supposed to be. Because of Jesus, because of his atoning love, he takes on all the guilt and corruption that we inherited in Adam and makes all things, including ourselves and our nature, whole and good and glorified, ready to live with our Savior for eternity.

> The LORD is exalted, for he dwells on high;
>> he will fill Zion with justice and righteousness,
> *and he will be the stability of your times,*
>> abundance of salvation, wisdom, and knowledge;
>> the fear of the LORD is Zion's treasure. (Isa. 33:5–6)

I repeated Isaiah 33:5–6 many times in hospice care, and many other verses of comfort. My mom started to speak in ways that combined with the here and now what appeared to be hallucinations, sometimes inserting Scripture. Once, her eyes opened wide and hard, and she lifted her head from the pillow (which commanded herculean strength) and said: "Why is this taking so long? I'm ready to have my robe of righteousness" (Isa. 61:10). Mom was hungry for heaven, and she knew what this meant. But as Mom waited—and as we wait—God promises that if Jesus is your Lord, he will be "the stability of your times." Dying is not a stable process. The body breaks down in bits and pieces. Each new day and each new hour bring new problems. And as your flesh disintegrates, if you are in Christ, your soul strengthens. And during this process—which would be frightening beyond belief without the Lord—God promises to be the stability of your times. And that is why the fear of the Lord is the beginning of wisdom (Prov. 9:10). Because only God gives us the stability of our times in the midst of the storm. And dying is a stormy process. It's stormy for the person who is dying, and it is stormy for those of us who keep on living.

Those eight days in hospice care gave us—Mom and me—time to do soul work together. We prepare for our heavenly home by recognizing that only two things will last forever: our souls and God's Word. Those eight days in the hospital allowed us to say,

"I love you."

"I know you love me."

"Do you forgive me?"

"I forgive you."

I know it takes a lot of faith to believe this. A week after her death, I was thinking out loud to a homeschool mom friend. I said something like, "I think my mom died in the Lord. But maybe it was the morphine talking?" She offered a gentle rebuke. Taking my eyes in her gaze, she said, "I'll bet people didn't really believe that your conversion was real at first either. It takes faith to believe that God saves sinners, doesn't it?" Yes. That is the point: it all takes faith. And faith is a gift from God. Faith, Hebrews 11:1 declares, "is the assurance of things hoped for, the conviction of things not seen."

A week after my mom's death, I was talking to some Christian graduate students at Duke University, right around the corner from where I live. At some point, I said something that, within the passing of a week, had become a potent and depressing lie. In answer to a student's question, I said: "Kent and I and some of our children are the only believers in our family." And then I paused. I stumbled and said, almost to myself, "No. That's not true anymore. My mother came to faith two days before she died. My mother is also a believer. My mother beat me to heaven."

My mother's salvation not only changed her future, but it changed our past as well. All the gory details of our past now live under the hue of God's providential hand. Each heartache a kiss from the Lord. A lifetime of feeling like I will never measure up melted into the tapestry of persevering faith. Hope heals. Faith remakes us. It really, really does.

8

The Daily Grind

The Basics of Hospitality

January 1, 2017, Durham, North Carolina

It really was a simple task, and not one I even spent a whit of time praying about.

My neighbor Shae, who runs the children's programs at the local YMCA, was going out of town, and I and another neighbor, Skylar, were taking care of her cats for a week. Tigger, the large and hospitable striped tabby, needed to take pills twice a day. While pilling a cat is not my favorite activity, it is a skill set in my arsenal. I had the morning shift, and Skylar had the evening shift. Because the task was a small and minor one—pill the cat, scoop the poop, make sure the other cat remained inside for the week, refill the food and water, and take in the mail—it did not bother me that I did not know either of these neighbors terribly well.

We can love our neighbors by pilling their cats, right?

Ordinary Hospitality Cares about the Things That Neighbors Care About

When I keyed into the house at six thirty on the Lord's Day that brought in 2017, I knew something had gone terribly wrong.

161

There were piles of a bloody body fluid deposited throughout the house, and Tigger was twisted in a fetal position, laboring to breathe, and looking miserable.

I got on my knees and stroked his warm head and felt his abdomen.

Being the gracious elder statesman that he was, he tried to lift his head to me, to show me that he appreciated a good head rub, even in his compromised health.

It was clear that he was a very sick cat.

I texted the owner and got no response.

I texted Skylar and told her about Tigger's condition.

I walked through the house, using all of Shae's paper towels to clean as much of the mess as I could. I bent over Tigger again and told him that he was a good cat. And then I left for home and church.

Our Lord's Days are full, and I did not return to Shae's until three thirty. By that time, Skylar had texted back and expressed dire concern, explaining that she was not able to come over until later that night.

By Sunday night it was clear that Tigger was dying. Shae, I learned, was out of the country and unable to access her text and email messages. Skylar and I were responding differently to this unfolding tragedy. Skylar, a vet tech by training, knew that Tigger needed to be euthanized. Tigger had, she felt powerfully, the right to die. I, on the other hand, did not have (1) freedom of conscience, or (2) permission by the law of North Carolina, or (3) the money in my checkbook to euthanize this cat. Our husbands came to Shae's house with all the kids and my friend Susanna. As we put our heads together about Tigger's welfare, we accidentally left the back door open, and Maisie, the other cat, escaped. Our motley crew redirected its energies to finding a frightened black cat on a cold, rainy night. After a hapless hour, we left. I prayed that the neighborhood fox wasn't hungry, and we said our goodbyes to one dying cat inside and one lost cat outside.

Once home, I collapsed defeated at the homeschool table, head in hands. Seeming to know my heart, my husband uttered: "This really is a quagmire."

"No kidding," I sighed. "One cat is dying and the other is lost. I'm a great pet sitter."

Kent looked perplexed. He shook his head, and he said, "No, no, no, not the cat thing. I mean dinner. We are in a quagmire. *What is for dinner?*"

Susanna and the kids burst into gales of laughter.

Kent had what we call his "Pa face" on; he looked guilty but also resolute in keeping the basics in the forefront. Dying cats notwithstanding, the man wanted food!

I rolled my eyes. Lentil soup was in the fridge and leftover Communion bread on the counter. The soup simply needed to be moved to the Crock-Pot, and the bread, which I had made yesterday, sliced and put into the basket. While unloading the dishwasher and directing the kids to set the table, I asked, "Which freezer should I use for the body?"

"What?" Kent looked appalled. "What body?"

Susanna had that good-Southern-girl-raised-in-a-good-Baptist-church look on her face. She muttered something like, "Only in this house do we face these problems."

"Guys, if he dies overnight, we have to put Tigger's body in the freezer. He won't likely make it through the night. And I can't use Shae's freezer, especially if I am unable to contact her during this week. Come on, she can't walk in the door and find her favorite cat in the freezer!"

We really were in a quagmire. Truly, if we didn't love our neighbors and didn't try to help, we wouldn't be making freezer space for a dead cat.

Skylar didn't sleep that night, as the thought of Tigger suffering alone was morally appalling to her. Her text messages recorded her misery. She had small children at home and a cat-allergic husband, so she could not do as she wished: go and sleep on the bathroom floor with Tigger and hold him while he died. I lived closer and had more mobility to do this, but even if I had felt compelled, Kent would have been my sanity keeper.

I know that hospitality is not just moral posturing. I know that hospitality is loving your neighbor at every opportunity and at every cost. I had allotted—generously, I had believed—thirty minutes each day to care for, pill, feed, and clean up after these cats during my neighbor's vacation. But twenty-four-hour cat crisis management, and neighbor-worldview-clash-grief ministry on top, well, this was simply not on my list of things to do.

I got up early on Monday morning, as I usually do, and after devotions and coffee and prayer, I walked in the dark, cold drizzle to Shae's. Maisie was mewing at me from under the back deck. Praise God! She shot in as soon as I opened the door and proceeded to dry herself on the couch before I could grab a towel. I opened a can of Friskies Buffet, and Maisie belted me across the calf, open clawed, before settling down to her breakfast. That's "thank you" in cat speech.

I braced myself and opened the bathroom door, expecting to find Tigger dead. He wasn't. He was lethargic, and more puddles of bloody excretion covered the bathroom floor and towels. I scratched his head, and he rested it heavily in my open hand. I sent a group text message about Tigger's condition, cleaned up the bathroom, and went home to call the vet.

It was a holiday (the Monday after a Sunday New Year's Day), and the only vet open was Vet Emergency. I called. The receptionist confirmed what I knew: euthanasia required written consent from the owner, and the cost was going to exceed $300. The vet on call told me that Tigger would really benefit from hourly administration of water from an eyedropper and maybe some Gerber baby food chicken from my finger. I sent out another group message, grabbed my eyedropper, dropped by a neighbor's who was likely to have baby food, and then headed back to Shae's. I felt very bad that Shae, who was of course on our group text-message thread, would be bombarded the moment she turned on her phone.

Kristin's boys met us at Shae's house. They are ten and twelve and are Knox and Mary's best friends. As I was administering water to Tigger, I heard commotion in the living room. I heard dogs barking manically and Knox saying, "Please don't let Maisie out, Miss Emily!" To no avail. Emily walked right in the house with her two small, yapping dogs, springing at the very tip of their leashes and collars, while Maisie dashed out the door. Really, who could blame the cat?

Emily is a dear neighbor who goes everywhere with her dogs. Shae's house is her safe space. So of course she would show up now. I was terse. I was harsh. I told her that Tigger was dying and that we couldn't have the dogs here. She looked hurt by any suggestion that her dogs were not welcome and told me under no uncertain terms that her dogs are gentle and good. She left quickly. She felt dejected. And I felt like a heel.

And then Shae texted. She was heartbroken. She wanted Tigger euthanized, and she wanted his ashes. She thanked us for holding him together until she could get phone service and think this through. *We didn't hold him together*, I thought to myself.

Skylar was at work and couldn't go with me to Vet Emergency. I did what I often do in an emergency: I called Kristin.

Kristin is one of the best bridge people I know. She makes friends easily and across all worldviews and political positions. At her fortieth birthday party, dozens of women from all seasons of life called her "mentor" and "friend."

Together we went into action.

Kristin's mom took all the children out for breakfast; Kristin and I took Tigger to Vet Emergency.

Throughout the process, Shae was texting me with goodbye instructions for Tigger. I got down on my knees with this precious dying pet and said all the things Shae wanted me to say, that he was a good cat, that she loved him, that she would miss him, that she had counted the rings on his tail while she nursed her own babies.

And then we were presented with the bill.

Did you know that the needle costs $350 on a holiday?

We had overspent on hospitality that month. And we did not have the money in the checking account.

Kristin paid the bill because I could not afford to.

We prayed, we laughed, we cried, and we lamented about why we always bond over emergency ministry efforts. We met up with the children and Paula (Kristin's mom) at Elmo's, and Paula sat us down at a table, put menus in our hands, and said she was paying the bill for breakfast and taking the kids home so that we could talk some more. And we were refreshed by good food and each other's faithful Christian company.

Later that night, after homeschool and dishes were done, I went back to the house to let Maisie back in. She and I replayed the script from the morning: angry, wet cat slashes incompetent pet sitter before settling down to a sensible can of savory chicken and vegetables. Then I texted Emily and asked her forgiveness for speaking to her harshly. She thanked me, forgave me, and then came over with the dogs to give me a hug.

———

Christian hospitality cares for the things that our neighbors care about. Esteeming others more highly than ourselves means nothing less. It means starting where you are and looking around for who needs you. It means communicating Christian love in word and deed. It means making yourself trustworthy enough to bear burdens of real life and real problems.

Radically Ordinary Hospitality Works from Strengths and Interests

My friend from church, Vicki, is a vibrant and engaging young mom. Her two daughters are five and two. When her family moved into a new neighborhood last year, she asked for prayer because she wanted to be hospitable. But with two young children, it is really hard to know where to start or how much you can commit to doing. So Vicki started by doing what she likes to do—art and crafts and memorizing Scripture set to song—and invited other mothers of young children in her neighborhood to join her.

First, she invited the neighbors on her block to come over on Tuesday morning for stories and Bible memory. She hand-made invitations, and she and her daughters walked them around the cul-de-sac. That was it. The first Tuesday, one neighbor and her daughter came.

The following week she invited some on surrounding blocks and those on her cul-de-sac to come back. Each week her gathering got bigger, and each week she invited more neighbors to come. Walking and praying around the whole neighborhood with a double stroller was good exercise and gave her a good feel for the different houses and people who inhabited them.

She now has about fifteen moms and children who attend. After stories and games and Scripture memory, the moms help one another by organizing grocery shopping and childcare trips for the week. Some of these moms are believers; others are not. A Tuesday morning Scripture and song memory for kids has turned into an all-day, neighbor-helping-neighbor day as, after Bible and songs and lunch, the women take turns going to Sprouts while others watch the children.

Vicki and I coteach Sunday school at our church. We love Dana Dirksen's Bible memory and catechism music.[1] Vicki uses Dana's music for her Tuesday morning group, which has become more than just a Tuesday morning group. The moms identify with Dana, and the gospel has become accessible and present to people.

After a while, the moms in Vicki's Tuesday group wanted to learn more about Jesus. Vicki picked up Jen Wilkin's book *Women of the Word*,[2] and soon some of the moms started asking if they could get together and read some and pray for each other. This started to gain traction too.

God was blessing the simple hospitality efforts of my friend who was looking around and praying for the people there, gathering them in close, and sharing the Word of God.

And every Tuesday morning I am on my knees for Vicki and her mom friends. Lord knows, moms of small children need help—the enduring help of the Word of God and of sisters in the Lord locking arms together and drawing others to him.

Radically Ordinary Hospitality Looks Out for the Old People

Donna came to me last summer and said, "When I'm an old lady, I want to walk to a Bible study once a week. So I think we should start this sort of thing now."

We live in a neighborhood with a number of older women, so many that the cul-de-sac at the end of our block is called "Widow's Corner."

Donna is also the best Bible teacher I know. And I know some fancy good ones.

Donna invited me and Sally to her house, and the three of us decided to divide up the parables of Jesus. Donna is not only an accomplished Bible teacher; she is also a great mentor and encourager. She wanted me and Sally to do our part, to use our own distinct voice and gifts, but not to forget our audience. We divided up texts and days, and the neighborhood back porch Bible club was started.

At the first meeting we had five women. They knew each other only to say hello and to check on one another's gardens. Reading the Bible together is intimate business, and one of the first questions that Hazel had was this: "If I disagree with everything you say, can I still talk?"

These were sweet, little, old Southern ladies, the kind who get their hair done once a week. And they were also deep waters, with hopes and fears and dreams and needs.

Each week the group got bigger, and warmer, and soon our lives started to intertwine. We prayed for each other throughout the week. Sometimes we walked together in the morning. We set up a meal rotation for Beatrice when she had surgery.

Over the years, friendships have deepened. Some are believers, and some are not. Some have been hurt and betrayed by the church, and this has taken a big toll. Others live alone and have benefited from having neighbors close at hand to check on them daily. This effort on Donna's part blessed us all. As Donna says, we also want to walk to a Bible study when we are old.

Donna just did what she does best—she is a great Bible teacher. And she is sensitive to the needs of older women in our neighborhood. She just opened her arms wide and drew others in.

Radically Ordinary Hospitality Relocates to Neighborhoods Hit Hard by Drugs and Crime and Poverty

You have already met Ken and Floy Smith, the pastor and pastor's wife the Lord used in my conversion. In 1975 Ken Smith pastored the Covenant Fellowship Church, located in Wilkinsburg, Pennsylvania, in a poverty-stricken community taken over by drugs and gangs and violence. Ken and Floy valued hospitality and community building, and having been discipled under both Billy Graham and Dawson Trotman (founder of the Navigators), they lived out the gospel with big plans. So when they left a mission field because Ken was called to pastor a church in a rundown community, they focused on outreach and community building. Weekly Bible studies were called "area fellowship groups," and everyone belonged somewhere. Church members started buying houses and duplexes and moved into—not away from—this crime-riddled area. Singles rented rooms with families, and a strong community based in love of Jesus, discipleship in the Word, and outreach developed and thrived throughout the 1980s.

In 1987 my friends Drew and Lynne Gordon moved into Wilkinsburg. The neighborhood was worsening—it was growing in poverty and crime and drugs and gangs. Drew and Lynne moved in, just as many people in the church moved out. Lynne recalls the identity crisis and fear: raising three young children in a home and hearing rounds of gunfire outside the front door rattled nerves and resolve. This was gang warfare, and no one knew how to stop it.

The church lost fifty members as it struggled with how to survive. The church needed meaning and purpose in order to serve in a neighborhood that it didn't understand. Then, when it looked like things couldn't get worse, they did: Ken Smith left Covenant Fellowship Church to pastor a church in Syracuse, New York. I'm glad he did, because, even though I didn't know it at the time, I really needed him, as I explain in *Secret Thoughts of an Unlikely Convert*.[3] But the church in Wilkinsburg was left without an undershepherd.

Why did Drew and Lynne and a small handful of others stay at the struggling church and in this impoverished and crime-riddled neighborhood? Because God was faithful, and Drew and Lynne and the families who stayed felt called to do so. They had a complex love for the church and the people who lived nearby.

A few years later, another pastor was called to Covenant Fellowship Church, and a local seminary student offered to start a program at the church called KidZone. He felt called to urban ministry. The seminary student was faithful and kept KidZone simple: every Tuesday night the church offered pizza and games and Bible stories for the children in the neighborhood. KidZone really took off, and the neighborhood started to rely on it. It became a vital link between the church and the community. When the seminary student graduated and left, the Butlers took up KidZone. Running such a program takes love and faith and sacrifice.

And that is how the church found its stride: by serving and getting to know the children in this neighborhood hit so hard by drugs and gangs and violence. The relationships formed with the children forged a way forward. It also humbled church members to know in intimate detail how poverty causes children to suffer. Who knew? Jesus, that is who: "Let the little children come to me and do not hinder them, for to such belongs the kingdom of heaven" (Matt. 19:14).

Is this just another do-gooder church? No. This is a conservative Bible-believing church that values the Westminster Confession of Faith. But it does value doing good.

As the church gathered momentum and focused on discipleship and caring for neighborhood children, another ministry developed: Wilkinsburg Christian Housing (WCH). It came out of the congregation's prayers for a way to make decrepit houses livable. Wilkinsburg is known for its abandoned buildings and homeless population. So WCH was formed and began to buy, restore, and rehab shells of houses left in disrepair and then used them for ministry and living. Between KidZone and WCH, the church was energized. The church became a place where the community could look for help. It launched community cleanup days, put in community gardens, established prison ministries, and watched as the Lord added to the kingdom.

In 2014 Covenant Fellowship called Peter Smith to be its pastor and to help give focus and organization to Wilkinsburg Christian Housing. Under Pete's leadership, the church has grown, and the WCH now has 501(c)(3) status.

Recently, the church planted twenty fruit trees beside the church building to help provide food for its neighbors. The community orchard and community garden cut a startling picture against the backdrop of broken concrete slabs of sidewalk, dug-up pavement, garbage, and graffiti.

The amazing Floy Smith went to be with the Lord on April 7, 2017. She was ninety-one years old. At her memorial service a month later, I wept and sang and embraced my old friends from Wilkinsburg. I sang psalms in four-part harmony, with Ken Smith at my right hand, at her memorial service, which was held at the Covenant Fellowship Church, with her son Pete, its pastor, presiding. I sang and worshiped and wept with people who prayed for me before I could pray for myself. And after a God-honoring memorial service, celebrating the life and home-going of a dear saint—a daughter of the King, my mother in the Lord—I sat out on Lynne and Drew's back deck.

The Gordons talked about how the neighborhood has changed over the decades that they have lived there. They talked about the gangs and the gunshots, and the prayer vigils that have taken back the night.

And as we looked to our right, we waved to and greeted the Smiths—Ken and his son Pete and the extended family drinking iced tea on the Smiths' back deck. Was it really seventeen years ago this month that Ken walked me down the aisle to marry Kent Butterfield? That seems like a lifetime ago. How faithful the Lord has been, to lead me into deeper union with him and deeper service to others throughout these years.

And when we looked to the left, we greeted the Butlers, an elder and his family in the church, also drinking tea on the back deck. And Wilkinsburg? The poverty is still there. The crime is still there. The gang violence has decreased, but it is still there. And yet here this house is surrounded by praying Christian neighbors—Christian neighbors who share a church and Christ's blood, and who prayed for their neighborhood and stayed put even when it was hard.

On the Gordons' deck I shared an orange with a radiant, young Christian woman who lives with the Gordons and attends a nearby college, studying opera. The Gordons first met her in KidZone. They were strangers once. And then they were neighbors. And now they are family of God.

And that is what radically ordinary hospitality accomplishes in the Lord's grace. It meets people as strangers and makes them neighbors; it meets neighbors and make them family.

Radically Ordinary Hospitality Includes the Children and Values Their Concerns

After my neighbor Hank was taken to jail, the cleanup of a meth lab began to take place in real time, right before my eyes. The front door of our house faces his, so we witnessed each gory detail. There was no turning a blind eye to the destruction and the devastation. Meth is toxic, and anything not nailed down in that house—and even some things that were—had to be removed. Seven Dumpsters of personal belongings were hauled from the house. And then, after the cleaning, came the washing of the walls, over and over, followed by more testing of the air and walls by the state department of health.

Cleaning up a meth lab is also a circus, and we had the usual string of cars driving in from other neighborhoods to loiter and watch the cleanup process. For weeks, the crime scene tape sequestered the lawn (or what was left of anything that remotely resembled a lawn after all of Hank's compulsive digging of holes and the heavy-booted police drama of removing Hank and Aimee with all the drug paraphernalia). We were told that the waste left over from the making of crystal meth had leeched into the yard and woods and that it was unsafe to walk there. Nonetheless, gawkers walked right into the open garage through the woods and front yard. They perused the contents of any open door. They picked through yard equipment. They acted as though they were attending an estate giveaway, and it was all for the taking.

It felt as though Hank's addictions and his crime were being exposed over and over again. If Hank had been Boo Radley incarnate when he lived here, he transformed into a larger-than-life ghost when he was taken from us.

My children were transfixed. And horrified. And so were the neighbor children who gathered with us. Tank, Hank's dog that came to reside with us, became the beloved neighborhood pet. Children fawned over him. Neighbors took turns walking him. Large bags of dog food showed up on our porch. Loving the dog became one way we all grieved for Hank.

The people hired to clean up the mess hauled away seven Dumpsters of Hank's personal belongings and his prized possessions. They trashed every single thing he owned.

The spectacle of Dumpsters prompted my children to pepper me with unanswerable questions, questions about loss and grief.

"Mom, where is Mr. Hank's toothbrush?"

"Mom, did they take the pictures that I drew for Mr. Hank last Thanksgiving, the one of the red fox in our woods?"

"Mom, did Mr. Hank eat the chocolate Easter bunny I gave him last year, or is that in the Dumpster now?" (Yes. Guaranteed he ate the chocolate. Hank is no fool.)

"Mom, why did they have to trash Mr. Hank's drum set and his guitars?"

My children and the children in the neighborhood who gathered with us wanted to know everything, including where Mr. Hank's belongings would be trashed: If his toothbrush is toxic and dangerous here, isn't it also toxic and dangerous in the dump? If it is toxic in solid form, if it is burned, doesn't it become more so? How do the stain and danger go away? Why do other people have to bear the burden of our toxic garbage? Our neighbor's house became a platform to discuss everything from drug addiction, the penal justice system, waste management, original sin, and environmental protection.

Children wanted to know—and I did too—why people who do not commit violent crimes bear decades of incarceration.

They wanted to understand what *addiction* means.

Questions spilled faster than Dumpsters could be filled with our friend's possessions.

A generational divide opened up in the neighborhood. If adults were clenching their fists over crashing property values, the Dumpsters of treasures humanized Hank to the children. They felt the pain, the pathos of it, in ways that no one else did. The police and others did their best to make Hank seem like a monster. But the sadness of losing a drum set and a dog was not lost on children. Regularly I would find a child weeping as another Dumpster was filled or moved.

Summer makes for long, hot days. The trampoline, woods, pond, popsicles in an outside freezer, and spectacle of the Dumpsters drew the neighborhood children to us. Knox and Mary have, of course, their own style of practicing hospitality. It involves using my Pampered Chef kitchen cups in the mud for the making of mud pies (Mary). It includes bringing snakes, chipmunks (usually the stunned and injured ones), and toads into the house for better observation or to share with our nature-deprived indoor cat

(Knox). Once, Knox brought a black snake into my bedroom and placed it on my pillow so that Caspian the cat could have a little visit. Another time, Mary found mating toads stuck together in twos in the pond. She scooped up some and brought them into the homeschool room and put them on our school table. Then she sang a skip-counting song that she had learned at Classical Conversations: "2, 4, 6, 8," sung to the tune of "Jesus Loves Me, This I Know." She shifted the curious lump of toads with a gentle hand. Nature adventures combined play and grief.

Kent and I observed how play is a vital part of grief. My children's hospitality to others had something to do with defending Hank's humanity. Kent and I witnessed the grief and the way that children rolled grief around with different worldviews about good people and bad people and how this all could happen here.

I started to pray that our home would also be a place for the children to grieve and make sense out of Hank's arrest.

We have always had an open door for our children's friends. Children know that they can get glasses of water or milk or Gatorade, have a snack from the snack cabinet, and ask for seconds from me. We aren't picky or stingy with children. I'm not fazed if a child polishes off the milk or the Pop-Tarts. We make ourselves available to listen to their concerns, but we don't get too involved unless blood or snakes are involved. (But because our house backs into the woods, blood and snakes are sometimes involved.) I have had to set rules about how many children can jump on the trampoline at the same time, or how much water can be used for water-gun fights. Recently I needed to remind the children that hand-to-hand combat on the Lord's Day violates the fourth commandment. (They actually asked me to defend my proof-texting that afternoon.)

Mary and Knox are central to our radically ordinary hospitality house, and they nightly invite their friends for dinner. Extra children join us not only for dinner but also for family devotions. But with the crime scene outside our dining room window, we were never very far from the grief that hung like heavy summer humidity and the object of questions and fear. Grief in the context of family devotions is a good combination. Children came for more than hot dogs and light-saber fights. Children wanted to talk through the crime, to make sense of it. They played and grieved in one exhale.

On a regular basis kids call home for permission to stay, and then they all set the table. We gather to eat and have Bible reading and prayer. It is always a mixed group these days. Some folks from church. Some from the neighborhood. Young and old. Some of these neighborhood children are churched, and others are not. Children have good questions—and they ask them forthrightly. We had to do some research to answer many of the questions they asked about the crime: What is crystal meth? Why is it so dangerous? Why do people go to jail for so many years? What does it mean to be addicted to drugs? Is addiction a crime? Does Mr. Hank have a pillow and a blanket? Sometimes we read from Hank's recent letter.

There is a powerful act of healing involved in seeing a problem through and having the eyes to see God's hand of direction and care for people. Even when God's providence is painful, it is purposeful. When the neighborhood meth addict and outcast becomes a brother in Christ, well, that changes everything. We quote Hebrews 13:3 a lot around here: "Remember those who are in prison, as though in prison with them, and those who are mistreated, since you also are in the body." When we remember that no one is out of reach of God's care, we heal in our grief.

This crisis has brought our neighborhood together, because Christ had already put Christians here to make sense of things. God never gets the address wrong. And after the Dumpsters were removed, after Hank's house was cleaned up and sold, our dinner table was left with the unmistakable imprint that comes from healing together with neighbors and children and Scripture and God's promises and prayer. I know that some people still talk about Hank as exemplifying what not to do, who not to become. But I— and the children—don't see it this way. We see Hank's humanity. And now we see faith.

I think that repentance makes you the very best role model you can be for children.

As they are getting older, the kids are eating a lot more. And they are helping each other and us more as well. We pray for them. We pray with them. We pray that they would grow to be stalwart men and women of God. And who knows: maybe one of those scrawny boys—maybe my son or one of his friends who built forts in our woods and ate us out of hot dogs and pizza—will grow in stature and faith and one day be my pastor.

Crazier things have happened.

9

Blessed Are the Merciful

The Hope of Hospitality

May 12, 2016, Thursday Afternoon

"The Butterfields knew Hank. They were friends. Could they have known about the meth lab?"

That is what our neighbors told the police that morning, when they arrested our neighbor Hank and his live-in girlfriend, Aimee, for cooking crystal meth in the basement.

All eyes were on us because we had worked hard to befriend Hank and to include this lonely man into the rhythm of our lives. He was not easy to win over. The truth is, although we had shared meals, holidays, and countless dog walks, it took a whole year before we knew his last name or had his permission to text him on his cell phone. But once we became friends, we loved and appreciated him. And he us.

After Mary and Knox helped find his missing dog, Hank trusted us. Hank said it best one day. He said, "You guys are my pack. That's cool."

Watching the DEA drag out Hank and Aimee from the scandal

and secret of their addiction was painful. Hank was ashamed, head low, not able to look at us. Aimee was flying high as a kite, her pink hair wild like her eyes. She made eye contact with me and waved. She blew kisses to my children, like a homecoming queen or a princess.

The police detoxed Hank and Aimee with less dignity than they gave Tank—fire-hosing them into sobriety, jerking them rag-doll roughly. Protected by white hazmat suits, they could treat them like subhuman trash. They thrust them on the ground like garbage when they were finished, leaving them to drip-dry where they landed. It was inhumane and wretched to watch. This is the process by which image bearers become prison numbers, lost people, nobodies. Hank was no longer our neighbor. He had become an object lesson about what not to be.

The police knew we were the neighbors who knew Hank best. By six thirty, we had provided them with Hank's mom's phone number. We told them that we would take responsibility for Tank, the enormous and depressed hundred-pound pit bull. One of the officers is a pit bull lover, and she was thankful that she could just hand Tank over to us. She said, "Pit bulls sprung from meth labs don't last long at the pound."

But now we were fingered as friends. Not just informed neighbors but friends of the evil one. That was true. And it cast us in a different light.

That the whole neighborhood accused us of loving this sinner was likely the best Christian witness we have ever had. But that doesn't mean it was pleasant.

By noon our house was like a trauma center, with the DEA and other members of the police team using our kitchen and bathroom and with neighbors coming by in a steady stream of concern, lament, and criticism. Tank was bathing in kid love and playing in the backyard with the other dogs. The world was compartmentalized by snapshots of normal (kids, dogs, forts, frogs) and insane (crime scene tape; neighbors complaining to the media about housing prices that would surely now plummet; Hank, shivering in the warm day, dripping wet from the shame of a public bath). By one o'clock, the DEA left our kitchen for good and returned to Hank's place.

Before they left our house, they warned all neighbors to stay inside. When they opened all windows and doors at Hank's house, the noxious toxins would be released into the air we breathe, and it would not be safe for us until six o'clock that night. Especially given the proximity of our house to Hank's, the warning given was stern. Grief and sadness and anger mingled with the tangled feeling of entrapment. People were fuming.

Bill, pacing in my kitchen and finishing up the last of the coffee from the morning, said, "I can't believe you could be friends with him! You want to know the problem with you Christians?"

No, Bill, I'm thinking, *but you are going to tell me anyway.*

"You Christians are so open-minded, your brains are falling out of your ears!"

It takes God's grace to get your neighbor to polish off the last of the coffee and insult you in the same breath.

Sissy, a sweet older woman, just held me and cried.

"That evil drug addict almost killed your sweet family!" she sobbed, her Carolina drawl adding vibrato and forte to each vowel utterance, her bony shoulders convulsing with each inhale.

More than one neighbor asked, "Did you know about the meth lab?"

More than one neighbor declared, "You must have known!"

Others asked, "Did you call the police on him? How could you *not* have known?"

The jury was in: the neighbors hated Hank and were not so very sure how they felt about us, knowing that we called him our friend.

For the whole day, Kent and I were doing ad hoc grief counseling. Neighbors, neighbor kids, Hank's sad and anxious dog.

The press swarmed our neighborhood with relentless fixation, and we dodged them like a norovirus. Ours was the largest meth lab bust in Durham, North Carolina, and it was Big News. The press did what it does best: stirred up unrest and gossip and left neighbors feeling exposed and raw.

My son Knox was inconsolable. Hank was our friend. Hank knew where the red-shouldered hawks nested and where to dig for hibernating salamanders in February. He shared things Knox treasured. Knox spent the day trying to cheer up Tank, who, like most pit bulls, is a sensitive soul. Tank knew, more than we did, the horrors of the last couple of days, or longer. Tank was also grieving his only human master.

Knox consoled himself by texting with Uncle Christopher (Yuan), and playing Angry Birds and Line Rider with his friends from the neighborhood. Daughter Mary spent the day in tears, grooming the dogs for comfort and sewing potholders and doll clothes from fabric scraps.

The din of *Star Wars* and the hum of the sewing machine and the laughter of children trying to make the best of insanity formed the backdrop of angry, accusing, adult conversation.

By the day's end (which we thought would never come to pass), with kids and dogs tucked in together in one room—for company and moral support—Kent and I had the first moment of the day to look each other in the eye and try to piece things together. How could we have missed a meth lab across the street? Was Hank—gentle, scared, depressed, sweet Hank—a dangerous man?

After we prayed together, Kent turned to me and said, "Would you have done any of this differently?"

I knew what he meant. Our neighbors were fuming mad at Hank, and their anger was spilling over to us. Had we missed some important clue? For the past two years, our neighbors had been warning us about Hank. They just had a bad feeling about him, they would say. Were they right and we wrong? It sure seemed so.

"Not a thing. Jesus dined with sinners. So do we," I said.

"Right," Kent said. "Being known as a friend of sinners has an edge to it I hadn't felt before though. But it is a compliment, really. This is what Jesus does. But I sure feel the edge."

That edge was ours now, like it or not.

And here is the edge: Christians are called to live in the world but not live like the world. Christians are called to dine with sinners but not sin with sinners. But either way, when Christians throw their lot in with Jesus, we lose the rights to protect our own reputation.

We stayed up late that night writing two letters, one to Hank and the other to the neighbors.

Our letter to Hank said we were praying for him, and we wanted to be there for him.

Our letter to our neighbors, posted on the Nextdoor app, invited them to a cookout at our house the following Lord's Day after church. We knew our neighbors needed time and space to talk about what had happened, and we wanted to bring Jesus in to this daunting picture. We sent off the invitation that night.

The next morning, Knox and Mary started a hand-drawn newspaper column for Hank, entitled "Tank's Paws Up and Paws Down." It was hilarious, documenting Prince Caspian the orange tabby's utter disgust that we had just added another dog to the house. Paws down, as his cat angst came out in claws drawn and fur on edge, uttering vile and hostile cat cursing at Tank. Paws up was Tank's open access to the litter box that, we learned the hard way, Tank mistook as a sandy tub filed with Tootsie Rolls for his consumption.

We pledged to pray daily for Hank and to visit him if he would receive us, which was one way that we as a family applied faith to the dire facts. We wanted to stick this thing out with Hank, because Christian neighboring is the real deal. We wondered if Hank would let us in.

We put the envelope in the mail, and we waited to see if we would ever again hear from our odd, quiet, reclusive neighbor who was generous with his skilled labor and dog knowledge, and who harbored a deep, dark, cavernous secret.

May 15, 2016, the Lord's Day

At nine o'clock on the Lord's Day morning after the meth lab was found, neighbors began to bring things over for our cookout. We left for church while neighbors set up tables and lawn chairs.

Shortly after three o'clock we arrived home from church. Almost the whole church came home with us, just as they had two years prior, after the robbery. It always helps to have Christians on hand to help people make sense of trauma.

When we arrived home, our front and back yards looked like an outdoor graduation party or wedding, green grass covered with tables and chairs, coolers and blankets. It was very inviting. We weren't sure if we were guests or hosts. It was vividly comforting to be enveloped by this presence. Familiar faces, open arms, bouquets of homegrown flowers clustered in a little girl's apron, a warm pan of home-baked beans in Sam's hot-pad-holdered hands. Our neighbors had softened. We were going to grieve this one together.

We embraced each other warmly. We were up to something sacred here.

After coolers of water and sweet iced tea were poured over bulky bags of ice and Kent had placed the first pan of burgers and hot dogs, hot off the grill, on a red-checkered tablecloth, he gathered us to the front yard. Standing in the middle of the driveway, Kent delivered a combination of a sermon on loving your neighbor and a table blessing for the food. Kent spoke for all of five minutes, but it was a powerful five minutes. The men removed their hats, and we bowed our heads in prayer.

Hank was our neighbor, Kent said, and Jesus calls us to love our neighbors, all of our neighbors, both the ones who are easy to love and the ones who are not. Kent described Hank as a mild-mannered recluse who helped us chop down trees and find Sully when he escaped out of the backyard. Kent shared that Hank struggled with depression and anxiety and had served time in the Army. Kent warned us of the destructive power of gossip and of failing to forgive one another. He reminded us that drug addiction makes slaves of men, and he said that we were each capable of all kinds of sin. And Kent let it be known to all that the same power that raised Jesus Christ our Lord from the grave is bestowed on all those who repent and believe on him. Hank's story is not over yet. And neither is ours. Jesus saves sinners like us.

After we ate and kids were off with push-up frozen pops for water gun fights, playing cops and robbers in the woods, and jumping with wet clothes on the trampoline (making rainbows with each toss), Kent gathered us back to the driveway to talk. Some neighbors, "wroth" as the King James puts it, challenged Kent on his benign interpretation of Hank. Others worried aloud about property values. As adults talked, the children and the dogs flopped on the warm grass with the colorful push-up pops dripping down their arms. Tank rolled over on his back, giving all the children ample room to pet his belly or scratch him behind the ears or offer him a helpful cleanup lick of melting ice pops. High-pitched anger diffused into softer, lilting tones.

As the sun set, I brought out the coffee cups. People lingered over the sheer magic of coming together in tragedy and strife. We stayed there drinking coffee and picking at potato salad until it was too dark to see our forks.

Neighbors walked home in funeral procession, sore with shock but warm from the persevering companionship of empathy, from being in the company of people who understand, and from belonging to a tribe that had just experienced something together, something that will always bind us. Neighbors embraced as they departed.

Wiping runaway tears with the back of a hand, one neighbor told Kent that she had been a little girl in a Baptist church who had once believed what Kent said about Jesus saving sinners just like us. She hadn't thought about that in twenty years. She wondered if Jesus was still waiting for her. Another neighbor said that the pastor of his church had talked that morning about the meth lab in Durham but hadn't put a personal face on it—either the personal face of Hank or the personal face of Jesus. Another woman said that at work that week, someone had said that rotting in jail for life would be the just outcome for that awful meth addict. Another neighbor responded that Hank's Christian neighbors would stick with Hank, because that is what Christian neighbors do. It was a procession of hope, a vision of promise, a drop of expectation of something good coming out of it, even as yellow tape unveiled shame: a neighbor missing, a house quarantined by "crime scene." The hope of Jesus was proclaimed in an ordinary neighborhood barbecue.

January 7–8, 2017, Durham, North Carolina

Since Friday, we have been under a snow emergency, an odd Mardi Gras–type day here in the American South. For the past week, the weather has been the only thing people are talking about. The anticipation of snow is a sweet blessing in the South, and a legitimate prediction of snow has been on the horizon. How many inches? How cold will it get? The young and the old have been glued to the news. My children's primary prayer request has been, "Let it snow!"

Snow started to fall at four o'clock Saturday morning. By six o'clock Mary and Knox were out of bed and begging to go to our neighbor's house. Kristin makes pancakes for the kids on snow days, and Ryan supervises their plummeting down the street on any flat surface they can find: laundry baskets, boogie boards, an old slab of linoleum.

Before the first drop of coffee had started to drip, local churches were canceling Sunday services, so Kent had asked me to invite all the neighbors over for family worship at our house. So I posted this on our Nextdoor app:

Dear Neighbors,
Because of hazardous road conditions, many of our church services will be canceled tomorrow (including the First Reformed Presbyterian Church of Durham, the church that we attend and that Kent pastors). We are therefore inviting any

and all to join us for an informal church service at our house, at 10:30 a.m. on Sunday, January 8, 2017. We will sing some psalms and Kent will deliver a short sermon. Rosaria will have the coffee on and some soup in the pot. Stay safe and warm, and if you know anyone in our neighborhood who is in need of help, please let us know.
Blessings!
Rosaria

By Saturday afternoon the roads were *Southern bad*, which meant perfect for kids and sledding. Five inches had already fallen, and the children were over the moon. I saw hoards of them walking to the hill by Kristin's house with their boogie boards over their shoulders. Those with grandparents from the North were toting real sleds. I knew that they'd knock themselves out for a few hours and then migrate over here for hot cocoa and snow jumping on the trampoline and pelting each other and Sully, the three-legged wonder dog, with snowball fights. By five o'clock I would have a pile of children with snot frozen to their faces coming in for a meltdown. They would watch a movie on Netflix, dripping over the floor in the homeschool room, and a pyramid of wet, white athletic socks would emerge by the front door. I planned to put out the Arnica gel, because they would all need it. I would try to get socks in the dryer before Sully chewed holes in them, and I'd towel off children as needed. (Sully is not the kind of dog who eats socks. He just finds the taste of salt-sweaty kid feet irresistible).

Kent would check out the roads and shovel the car out, and then he would work on a short sermon for the neighbors. He had been praying about what to preach, about what would bring healing and saving grace and a knowledge of Jesus Christ as prophet, priest, and king.

I'd been praying that God would be honored by our worship on Sunday and that it would heal us. Many neighbors were still bitter about Hank and the meth lab he'd operated across the street and about the public shame that had descended upon us when the DEA arrested Hank eight months ago. It is hard to express the weight of a neighborhood locked in anger and shame. Such feelings pervade everything.

I marveled at the opportunity God had given us in our neighborhood to be candid and direct, even if we were disappointed in one another's responses. It had become very clear that people can share the same experience in vastly contradictory ways. This neighborhood tension still weighed on my heart and on the hearts of my children. How would this all change? When it comes to change, Kent is fond of reminding us that we don't start with relationships or culture or things out there. We start with ourselves. We start where we are. We start as soon as we feel convicted by our sin. We start regardless of what the people around us do or don't do. As a neighborhood, we had been gawking at the big house surrounded by yellow police tape. It still drew rubbernecked drivers from other neighborhoods. Not only was it an eyesore; it pulled our gaze in the wrong direction.

On Saturday afternoon I cooked for Sunday while assessing the (unlikely) driving. My friend Susanna had a follow-up doctor appointment scheduled. (If you recall, she'd had eye surgery on Friday and was recuperating at our house. Poor girl. Our house is usually chaos, and my children consider Susanna the aunt of their dreams. Read: No privacy. No silence.) Five inches of snow in Durham is equivalent to twenty-five inches of snow in Syracuse. And the snow was still falling. There would be no plow until Monday morning at the soonest. Often in the South, the snow strategy is to wait it out until it melts.

I was confident that we would have people in our home the next day, sitting under the worship of God and singing the Psalms, among them those who would never of their own volition walk through the doors of the First Reformed Presbyterian Church of Durham. Kent and I have been doing this for sixteen years now: anticipating a big group in our home for worship when inclement weather prohibits getting to the church. For all the years of marriage and ministry, Kent has never viewed a weather-related church cancellation as a day off. Never once. A snow day is a day *on* for Kent in a special and spiritually rigorous way.

Now, Lord's Day morning has arrived, and icy snow blankets the terrain. Our backyard, our front yard, the green picnic table, and the tire swing are frozen in place like a domesticated gorge. The street is a sheet of ice, and so is the driveway. We had invited everyone connected to our Nextdoor app—potentially three hundred households. There was so much to do.

So I pour my coffee and open my Bible—I use a one-year Bible for morning devotions—and I begin with prayer: "Dear Father, please open my eyes and heart by your Spirit, that I might see the glories of your Son in every detail that unfolds by your providence today." After reading my daily selection from the one-year Bible, I next turn to *Tabletalk* magazine, followed by five psalms (Psalm 8 [because it is January 8], 38, 68, 108, 138) and Proverbs 8. I open my Psalter and sing. Then I pick up my knitting needles. I'm making some wool socks for my friends in Chicago. I open my journal to my intercessory prayer list and begin to pray as I knit my rounds and rounds of ridges and rows.

After devotions I go to the kitchen. I had baked the bread and soaked the beans the night before, so I now get to the business of cooking for a crowd. I always cook for a crowd, so this morning is no different from other mornings except that I really didn't know who will show up. I make Brazilian black bean soup (from *The Moosewood Cookbook*), Indian dhal (from a recipe in my head), and short-grain brown rice. I chop red peppers for the salad and then put on a pot of oatmeal for breakfast. As I cook, I listen to a Psalms CD, *Refuge: Selections from the Book of Psalms for Worship*.[1] I recognize the voices from decades ago. There is Ron, sturdy and dynamic in his resonating baritone voice. Somewhere behind Ron, I can discern Shari's lilting soprano. As the soups burbled, the songs of Jesus envelope me in an embrace that is both ancient and personal.

Kids up, breakfast done, dogs fed, and Monopoly game (the Jurassic World edition) are removed from the coffee table that will become a makeshift pulpit. Kent prays, and I start the big percolator.

What happens next is drop-dead sacred.

My beloved neighbors walk through the door for worship: Missy; the two Millers; Ryan and his son Ben; the three Mutters; Maeve; the five Shepherds; the two Harviews; and the five McKenzies. Susanna is here, recovering from Friday's eye surgery. She can't see, but she finds her way upstairs via Mary's guiding hand, and we put her in a comfy chair. Daughter Mary says that Susanna is now like Mary in Laura Ingalls Wilder's *By the Shores of Silver Lake*, when scarlet fever settles into her eyes and makes her blind. Fortunately for Susanna, in reality, she has just had elective PRK laser surgery and will soon have better vision than any of us after a few blurry weeks.

I'm boiling and decanting water into the big thermos, for tea and hot cocoa. Then I start a search for the mini-marshmallows (I hide them from the kids, and I have hidden them so well that a few shelves in the pantry are getting an impromptu organizational redo). The kids are embracing their friends and finding places to put coats. Bella, the small and elegant shih tzu, will soon be burying herself in the coats left on the floor. Kent and Bob count chairs. Mary Beth brings a big pot of soup, and we add that to the stove. Bless her. We needed another pot. We gather mugs and smiles and press cold cheek to cold cheek. We are neighbors. Donna and I lock arms and eyes, and she whispers, "This is bigger than my dreams." We are Protestants, Catholics, unchurched, young, old—all together under one roof, one Word. One set of neighbors looks across the room to see an older lady for whom they have been praying for two decades. They have longed to see her in church, in Christ. The barriers to both seem insurmountable on most days. But the Lord, who numbers and names the stars—who "heals the brokenhearted and binds up their wounds" and "determines the number of the stars" and "gives to all of them their names" (Ps. 147:3–4)—also heals broken hearts. And so here she is. And here they are, to behold the fruit of their prayers. Miracles are already surrounding us.

Kent welcomes everyone and reminds them of the powerful

role that Jesus bestows upon neighbors. From the big window, we can still see the police tape surrounding Hank's house. Kent goes right there: "Jesus calls us to forgive, because without forgiveness, we cannot be agents of grace or in the path of grace." Kent asks me to lead us in singing, and as we sing, I watch the faces of my neighbors.

The melody for the psalm we sing is "Crimond"—and for those musically trained, this Welsh rendition is familiar and elegant. We go slowly. We savor how mere words weave reassurance: "The Lord's my Shepherd, I'll not want; / He makes me down to lie in pastures green, he leadeth me, the quiet waters by." The waters outside are frozen, and the green picnic table looks encased under water. "My soul he doth restore again, and me to walk doth make, within the paths of righteousness, ev'n for his own name's sake." I savor each word. Each soul. Each promise. "Yea though I walk in death's dark vale, yet will I fear no ill; for thou are with me and Thy rod and staff me comfort still." My mind wanders to the documentary of Temple Grandin, a professor of animal science and an autism-rights leader. She studies cows, and she developed a system to move cows through a chute in order to make a slaughterhouse more humane. So paradoxical. So distasteful (to me, a mostly-vegetarian). But cows, Temple proved, are different from sheep. Cows must be prodded from behind; sheep must be led from the front. That's why we walk through death without fear: Jesus, our Shepherd, leads gently. "A table thou has furnished me in presence of my foes; my head thou dost with oil anoint, and my cup overflows."

Singing psalms with my neighbors in worship at our home is almost more than I can bear. God's Word rings realistic—God protects us in the midst of danger, not necessarily from danger. He says in Luke 10:3, "Behold, I am sending you out as lambs in the midst of wolves." We are singling slowly, more slowly than we do in church. Many are singing this for the first time. The words of Christ are sinking down, down, down. And then we conclude: "Goodness and mercy all my life, shall surely follow me;

and in God's house for ever more, my dwelling place shall be." We take a breath and look around. Singing psalms with neighbors is intimate business. When we sing a psalm together, we speak the truth of God's Word to one another, truth unhinged from our problems and peeves, maybe for the first time in our lives. People can be neighbors for twenty years and not do this ever.

Kent prays for our worship and asks God to be present with us, to work healing where healing is needed, repentance where repentance is needed, and salvation where salvation is needed. Kent doesn't mince words. He is not one man in the pulpit and another man in his home. As I watch him open the Bible, I am grateful that God allowed me to marry this man.

Kent's sermon is short and to the point. The passage he preaches from is Matthew 5:7, "Blessed are the merciful, for they shall receive mercy." It is short and to the point, but the hidden truth behind the beatitudes is that they were delivered to the disciples and require faith to execute. Kent tells our neighbors, "You can show mercy only if you know God's peace. If you are still mad at Hank, then you have spiritual work to do. Do you have God's peace? Have you made peace with Jesus? Do you know him? Have you repented of your sin and placed your hope in Christ alone?" And then Kent prays. He prays that we would be the neighbors that God has called us to be, for our own good and for God's glory. He prays for salvation where it's needed. He prays that God would help our unbelief.

After singing another psalm (Psalm 104, which is my favorite snow psalm), Kent gives the benediction:

> Now to him who is able to keep you from stumbling and to present you blameless before the presence of his glory with great joy, to the only God, our Savior, through Jesus Christ our Lord, be glory, majesty, dominion, and authority, before all time and now and forever. Amen. (Jude 24–25)

And after the benediction, Kent invites everyone to step into the "dining rooms" and enjoy pots of soup and warm bread and hot cocoa and coffee. My daughter Mary goes around and asks the dog owners to go get their dogs and bring them over to play with Sully in the backyard. Soon, the backyard looks like a kennel, and the house is buzzing with neighbors eating soup and warm slices of fresh bread. Snug aromas and singsong tones of neighbor talk promise good things.

We set places for twenty-five people, gathering around three tables. As is our usual, we use anything for chairs: kitchen stools and piano benches, and exercise balls fill in when dining room chairs run short. We make an assembly line, passing pots of soup through the narrow hallway. We ooh and aah over the warm bread that Maisie brought and the amazing white chicken chili that Tina serves. The children pile their plates high and fill their bowls deep and then head to the freezing back porch to eat without grown-ups. We talk about kids and snow and work, cancer and bad knees and politics. And then the talk moves to Hank.

"Kent, tell us how Hank is doing. I know that you visit him in jail," David offers, as the warm bread makes another round through the tables.

"Hank is fragile, of course. Jail breaks a man. But Hank has also just recently committed his life to Jesus. And Jesus will not let him down. Jesus will guide him through this. This is scary, of course, and so we pray and write a lot, and we place our hope in Jesus."

This is precious truth. It was something that Kent and I and the kids were still marveling over, and while we want to share this good news with our neighbors, we want to be careful to share it in a way that honors God and Hank. This is not cheap news. It is not the kind of news Kent would tarnish by bragging about it on a blog post or on Facebook. Kent is a Christian man. Christian men do not steal glory from God. This is the kind of news that moves mountains, something to be addressed in the sacred moment of table fellowship.

Quiet descends; a holy hush hovers over the table. Kent explains that Hank has been desperate for help, but there is no real, earthly help for him. Kent explains that Hank's arrest has opened the door to new, vital, and urgent intimacy between our family and Hank. There is no pretending otherwise: Hank needs Jesus, the rescuer, because no one else can go where he has been taken. He has detoxed from meth, and he is feeling completely, utterly lost. Hank does not need a life preserver or a pep talk. He needs to be rescued by God himself. Hank knows now that he needs Jesus—his Savior—to shepherd him through the long, dark days ahead. Hank was not raised in the church, so this is all very new to him. But he is reading his Bible daily. And he prays. He prays for all of us. He is thankful that we pray for him.

Kent is speaking softly now, and the room, once bursting with talk and laughter, is captive in silence. Kent explains that Hank is no longer the meth addict across the street but a brother in the Lord.

That captures the gospel in real time.

It is hard to explain what happens to a community when the local drug addict commits his life to Jesus. But I suspect you can imagine. It changes everything.

Slowly, people start to talk to each other again. We have finished most of the food, so cleanup is easy. We load the dishwasher and find coats and hats and boots. The children stay back to watch a movie and play in the snow. As shadows lengthen into dark, winter, late afternoon, neighbors reclaim their dogs and soup pots. Slowly we all pull back into our separate homes. We know that we have experienced something sacred: neighbors from all stripes coming together to worship God and break bread together. And Boo Radley is no longer the scary dude with tattoos and a mysterious addiction. He is my neighbor still, and he is made in the image of God.

———

I think back on that day a lot.

Our neighbors do too.

Months after this snow-day worship, one of my neighbors commented that when we walked from the living room into the dining room, and she saw the three tables set, ready for all of us, she had never felt so loved in all her life. She actually said that.

The fixings were simple: pots of soup and loaves of bread. A set table (mix-matched, of course, but still waiting and ready for whoever would come). The Word of God gathering people home.

Why is something this simple so very hard to do?

In *How to Survive a Plague: The Inside Story of How Citizens and Science Tamed AIDS*, journalist and author David France records an encounter between Cliff Callen and Richard Berkowitz, two men who were living with AIDS in the early 1980s, when testing positive came with a life expectancy of two years. When we meet them in this scene, Callen and Berkowitz are suffering under the lack of medical help and railing against the homophobia of mainstream America. As their conversation turns to what they think it will be like to die, Callen says to Berkowitz: "I can see that unlike most of the queens there, you are not ready to glamorize or embrace dying, and sick as I am, neither am I. I hope when my time comes that I can face it without turning to God or religion, because if I do, that would be a betrayal of everything I fought for and everything I believe in."[2]

While I was reading that book today, the stark power of those words made me gasp.

The greatest fear of a man standing on the brink of eternity was turning to the God who made him.

How would you listen if you were at a table having lunch with those two men?

What would you say?

Would you want to be at this table?

Why aren't we at this table, having lunch with these two men?

On our snow-day worship, the normal divisions that yawn wide for most of us ceased to exist.

Refugees and Terror

Later that month, on January 30, 2017, President Trump closed the borders to refugees for four months. All hell broke loose, both nationally and in my neighborhood.

My neighbors and I grieved differently over this, but we met over a meal at our house to discuss it. We had already broken ground on hosting, so when a crisis was presented, my neighbors knew it was safe to ask and safe to come and safe to cry. At home-school co-op, my neighbor Cassy asked me if I would host another conversation about politics. We did so the night before the election, and we prayed for our nation and for our friendships, fearful that our different positions could easily divide us. And different we were. Some neighbors at the gathering voted for Clinton, some voted for Trump, and Kent and I voted for neither.

Ty was fuming mad as she entered the kitchen, talking fast and furious about wanting to march, peppering her fury with, "Not my president!" Beth was more subdued, sad, wondering what we were to do next. Terry marched in with a sermonette, declaring that because Jesus was a refugee, any government and any people who support closing the borders to refugees are not being Christian. Some people agreed. Others did not. I'm friends and neighbors with people from both sides. It clearly was a divisive moment. It prompted Beth to muse, as she wept in my kitchen, "When people worship together, when people come to the Lord's Table together, does it matter if we believe the same things? If I believe in biblical marriage, and the person next to me in the pew believes in marriage equality, is that okay?"

Dinner was soup and salad and some amazing and enormous artisan bread from Whole Foods that Cassy had picked up. We gathered. We talked. We prayed. We fed our children, and we hugged. We leaned into this reality:

> God is our refuge and strength,
>   a very present help in trouble.
> Therefore we will not fear though the earth gives way,
>   though the mountains be moved into the heart of the sea,

though its waters roar and foam,
> though the mountains tremble at its swelling. Selah
> > (Ps. 46:1–3)

We remembered that God is our Creator, and that he is holy, and good, and sovereign:

> The LORD works righteousness
> > and justice for all who are oppressed. (Ps. 103:6)

There is something about grieving in the backdrop of God's Word. It makes you long for the power of God's Word—and fear it with a holy fear at the same time. The grief is still there. The fear that this world is exploding in angry divisions prevails. But more prominently there is God—our refuge in times of trouble.

There is something about grieving the fate of a worldwide refugee crisis that makes you know in a deep and seamless way that mankind is lost without Jesus. And Jesus, who died to redeem his people, gives us a steady guide, a fierce power, an inner peace, and a quiet resolve. The same power that raised Jesus from the grave he has given to those who have committed their lives to him, so that we can serve gospel peace and be a bridge to the Lord himself in this dark world. But there is much work to do.

Mercy brings it all together. God's mercy poured out on the cross, emboldening us to keep the door of our homes open to others.

Conflict in our neighborhood drew people in close—neighbor to neighbor.

Such drawing in does not replace the church—it brings the church to the people. It meets people with gospel grace where they are. It leaves them yearning for more.

There are, of course, other ways you can use your days, your time, your money, and your home. But opening your front door and greeting neighbors with soup, bread, and the words of Jesus are the most important. Who knows but that this simple task of sharing the gospel where you are, wherever you are, might just be used by God to change the world?

10

Walking the Emmaus Road

The Future of Hospitality

Spring and Summer 2016, Durham, North Carolina

That very day two of them were going to a village named
Emmaus, about seven miles from Jerusalem, and they were
talking with each other about all these things that had happened. While they were talking and discussing together,
Jesus himself drew near and went with them. But their eyes
were kept from recognizing him. And he said to them, "What
is this conversation that you are holding with each other as
you walk?" And they stood still, looking sad. (Luke 24:13–17)

This passage in Luke spills over with grace and care. Jesus models
here what the future of our daily, ordinary, radical hospitality is
all about.

First, Jesus does not come with an apologetics lesson. He comes
with a question. And then he listens compassionately as the two
share pain, disappointment, abandonment, betrayal. The pain in
their heart is extreme, so much so that they must stop walking to
compose themselves. And they don't just stop—they stand still.

199

The drama in the narrative halts with this reality: "And they stood still, looking sad."

They are going somewhere, but they don't know why. They lose their vision. A question derails them.

That happens to a lot of people.

Jesus does not hurry them. He does not jolly them. He doesn't fear their pain or even their wrong-minded notions of who the Christ should be or is. He knows that the process is important. He knows that grief and lamentation are vital to the soul. The Christian life isn't a math test. A whole lot more than the answer matters a whole lot more. So he accompanies them in their suffering. And we need to do the same. When people are willing to stop and tell us where they hurt, we need to praise God for it, and we need to stop what we are doing, shut our mouths, and listen with care.

The men tell their side of the story: Jesus was the Christ, or so they had believed. He was crucified. And on this, the third day, the tomb is empty, and angels have reported that Jesus lives. But when they looked into the tomb, all they saw was emptiness (Luke 24:19–23). Jesus, after hearing their side of the story, speaks words of grace, words that tell the whole story, words that expose the goodness of both law and grace. And that is what the Bible always does. It tells the whole story. And the whole story is one of multi-directional hope—of past and present and future, of what will come to pass, and of what must be fulfilled in order for hope to manifest.

Jesus tells his fellow travelers that nothing has happened apart from what the Old Testament prophesied: the sufferings of the Christ are the appointed path to glory. The Old Testament had prepared them to hear this, but the cross itself became a stumbling block. Severity. Humiliation. They knew their Scriptures, but seeing them in the backdrop of the cross was too much to bear. Because it is too much to bear. And that is why Jesus takes their hands—and ours—and walks with us. Grace does not make the hard thing go away; grace illumines the hard thing with eternal meaning and purpose. Grace gives you company in your affliction, in Christ himself and in the family of God. Matthew Henry writes:

> A golden thread of gospel grace runs through the whole web of the Old Testament. Christ is the best expositor of Scripture; and even after his resurrection, he led people to know the mystery concerning himself, not by advancing new notions, but by showing how the Scripture was fulfilled, and turning them to the earnest study of it.[1]

Jesus Christ is not a red-letter Christian, and this should be a stern warning to the rest of us. Jesus leads people to know the mystery concerning himself. On the Emmaus road he brings them back to the Old Testament, showing how the moral law of God, which existed at creation and is still binding, is for our good and for God's glory. Anything with "mystery" in it is a long conversation, delicious and slow and necessary, and it ought not be rushed. Matthew Henry writes: "Those who seek Christ shall find him: he will manifest himself to those that inquire after him; and give knowledge to those who use the helps for knowledge which they have."[2]

Those who seek Christ shall find him.

But, often, much must be rent from our precious grip before we seek. And when our dreams of the future are ripped from us, we must grieve. Godly grief makes a clearing for the Lord's healing balm of forgiveness, reconciliation, and restoration.

Aimee

A month before Hank was arrested, a bony, pink-haired woman named Aimee moved into his house. She had hollow cheeks and those open sores on her face common to all the drug addicts I have ever known. She mumbled soft hellos, eyes averted, head down.

After Aimee moved in, strange things started to happen.

Tank began running away again. He spent more and more time wandering the streets. Whole threads on the Nextdoor app went like this:

"Tank's out again."

"Does anyone know who the big, gray pit bull belongs to? I'm calling the dog catcher!"

"Something has to be done: I almost ran over that damn dog last night coming home from work."

One morning at four thirty, I opened the back door to take out the recycling, and Tank was just sitting there, waiting for me, with his soulful eyes boasting a story I was too dumb to read. I brought him in and fed him, and he curled up on the couch for a snooze. When Mary and Knox awoke, they loved on him. We walked him and played with him, and then tried to return him to Hank. We went over and rang the bell, knocked on the door, and texted, but no one answered us.

This became our ritual.

Hank stopped walking with us or working in his garden. We missed him.

Other strange behavior followed. Hank bought a brand-new truck. And the second day it was parked in his driveway, torrential rains came. Aimee left the passenger-side door open all night long, and a torrent poured in and through its seats and carpet, water drenching the wires. Ruined. It went from pristine new to broken trash in one act of carelessness.

Aimee loved children, or so she said, and talked with me about her sadness at losing custody of hers. One day she came over with two heavy black garbage bags full of clothes. She said that she was up all night thinking about our family and wanting to do something for us. So she went Dumpster diving on garbage day and found some clothes she thought would be perfect. She even found something for me. With the desire to please bubbling behind her sad, gray eyes, she declared: "I found you a cute little black shift, size 6. The hem hits just above the knees. It will look really classy on you when you go and give your lectures."

I gave Aimee a hug but sequestered the garbage bag in the carport, planning to stick it in the garbage as soon as I could do so without notice. Aimee felt hollow to the touch. Hugging her felt like killing her. She was bone thin and fragile. I pulled back.

The Lord's Day before the arrest, Aimee was standing in the front yard looking forlorn. I was returning from a dog walk, and she walked across the street to greet me. She looked awful—bony, open sores on her face, her thin, falling-out hair greasy and matted against her scalp and around the temples. Her empty eyes were red with exhaustion. She started to speak, but her voice was so raspy hoarse that I could barely hear her. I leaned in and instinctively recoiled. Her breath and body odor were noxious, worse than cigarettes and vomit. But I heard the request clearly:

"Rosaria, can I talk with you alone about something? Hank is being, um, weird. Something is wrong. Bad wrong," she said, using all of her might.

I'm ashamed to tell you what I said.

I said: "This is a tight week for me, homeschooling and travel. Can we talk next week?"

That's what I said.

Seasoned to rejection, Aimee took mine in stride with the lifetime that preceded it.

I thought nothing of my sin against her for the precious few days that it hung dormant in the air, yet unfulfilled.

Only when the DEA swarmed the house, dragging out my neighbors like pieces of trash, did the finger of God's conviction tap me on the shoulder. The good Samaritan went out of his way. I protected my time and space.

Watching the hazmat team suit up and tear through the front door, I remembered. My dodging of a conversation with Aimee came back with a force that only God's conviction of sin can give. And only then did I stop to ponder it. What did Aimee want to tell me? That she needed help? That they were cooking meth in the basement garden tub? Maybe she would have asked me to help her get out. Who knows? I will never know what she would have said. But this I know for sure: I could have helped, but I was too busy and too selfish to notice.

———

The letters that Hank writes from jail are gloomy, dark, depressed. Incarceration exacerbates his anxiety disorder, chronic depression, PTSD, and ADHD. A private and reclusive man by nature, public cells and public toilets violate all rules and limits of what counts as normal. He lives in fear every minute of every day. Detoxing from crystal meth is no picnic. The experience is breaking him—and the Savior he so recently and so weakly follows, the Word he weakly reads, and the prayer he weakly utters all point to the stark reality that God is appointing all of this. Waiting for the plea bargain from the district attorney who can't remember his name is more than he can bear on most days.

But write to us, he does.

And we write back.

Kent visits him in jail.

And we send him books.

We sent him the *NIV LifeHacks Bible* and self-care books and the novels I am reading to the children so that he can stay on the same page with us.

Christopher Yuan sent him *Out of a Far Country* with a note that said, "I understand," and Lynne and Drew Gordon from Crown & Covenant Publications sent other books about Christian living, with warm letters of welcome and belonging in the family of God.

Friends from church, friends whom he first met at our house on Thanksgiving or Christmas or Easter, sent letters and history books and writing journals. I pause and think about this a lot. God's providence preordained that Hank would spend holidays with the Christians who open arms wide and claim him. Where else would my meth-addicted neighbor meet his church family, apart from our table? Where would I have met my church family, apart from Ken and Floy's table?

When Hank has a good day, he writes a letter to Mary and Knox, thanking them for caring for Tank, thanking them for the good memories he has because of our dog walks, and thanking them for praying for him in jail. He closes his letters to my children like this: "Please pray that God will give me more grace to get through today. I want to get out so that we can take our dog walks together. Your brother in Christ, Mr. Hank." They always write back, saying things like, "Dear Mr. Hank. The fox is back in the woods, and the red-shouldered hawk babies have left the nest. So much is happening. Tank sleeps with me. I love you and miss you and pray for you every day."

I know for a fact that the only letters Hank has ever received from praying children who know him well have come to that hell called the county jail.

It's hard to love God when you see his hand holding up the bars.

Hank asks for prayer and letters and pictures. He thanks me for our dog walks. He thanks me for our conversations.

But one day, he made a special plea to me.

Hank wrote: "Rosaria, will you write to Aimee? She has no one. This was all my fault. And she needs help. She needs food."

When Hank made this request, I was spelling Aimee's name wrong (spelling it Amy) and I didn't know her last name.

Trauma forges lines of intimacy and second chances.

This was my second chance.

So I started writing to Aimee.

I started with an apology.

She wrote back immediately and with sincere gratitude.

In her first letter she asked me to pray for her children, that they could somehow forgive her for all she has done. She also asked me what I did with the clothes she gave to me. She told me that she went through every item of clothing, searching every pocket for fear that she might have left crystals of toxin behind. She told me she wanted to be safe and careful with me, and to try to protect me. "Remember," she wrote, "I am both an addict and a mother." She also asked for food—monthly food packages.

In jail the food is sketchy and sparse. And if the detox program meets when the mess hall is open, the meal is missed. And detoxing in hunger is sheer misery.

I sent Aimee an iCare package, selecting the one with the most canned meat. iCare is the program that manages food supplements for the county jail. They are expensive and sparse, but they are something.

Aimee started going to the church services held in jail, and she tried to read the King James Version of the Bible in the detention center. The words were hard and the print small, and she couldn't make any sense of it. She asked me if I would send her a Bible.

I sent a large-print women's devotional Bible the next day (New Living Translation), after Susanna helped me to do an Amazon search for a Bible that would suit her.

Aimee told me that she loved her new Bible. And the simple promises of the Bible, written in calligraphy in the first pages, the words of Jesus's love and faithfulness, caused her heart to ask: Could Jesus be my Shepherd too?

Aimee's next letter said that she needed help reading her Bible. Could I please send a book in which she could write her feelings about what God's Word means? But, please, could I find a simple book? Her head ached, she hadn't bothered to read print in years, and she'd never finished high school.

My friend Hope went on an Amazon hunt and found something perfect. In this particular jail, books and care packages must be vetted through either Amazon or iCare. Nothing can be sent from home. It's too risky. A family friend might slip a knife between the pages of the family Bible or cannabis in a home-baked blueberry muffin.

Aimee needed monthly iCare food-supplement packages and daily prayer. My children drew pictures for her cell, and I wrote about one letter to her every four. Aimee is an ambitious and prolific writer with a beautiful hand (hard to produce with the stubby pencils provided in jail) and a penchant for colorful notecards. Almost each card has had something written on the inside flap. One looked like a Bible-reading plan: "Genesis–Malachi." Another looked like a prayer request: "CGH in cell 5-S." Sometimes I can discern a name: "Clarissa 3-E Tarish Cell Block R." I don't know what those messages mean, so I just pray for any name I see written there.

Jail is rough. Detoxing is rough. Aimee waits seemingly indefinitely for the public defender to offer her a plea bargain. She feels forgotten and rejected.

When last month a young woman hanged herself in the cell next to Aimee's and the outcries of death fell on helpless ears and thoughtless guards, Aimee could not breathe or sleep or move. Life lingered at the precipice of a rope all night long. It turned out to be a seventeen-year-old girl.

I have a letter from Aimee on my desk that I hope to answer this week. This letter is hopeful. In it she writes: "I have been here almost a year now. I was thinking about you. So, I think I am doing okay for being here so long. God bless you, my friend. Tell everyone I said hello, and I send my love."

Before I could respond to that letter, another came in the mail:

> I have big news. I accepted a plea bargain for a ten-year term. It's called an "open plea," which means the judge decides how long. I hope I made the right decision. Ten years is a long time, but I plan to use my time well. I hope to finish my GED and get a job in prison. I'm not sad, so don't worry about me. I worry about Hank. And my children. I know ten years is long, but this is God's will. I have a lot more in my life now than I have ever had: I have sobriety, faith, salvation, and hope in God. Please give everyone my love. And thanks for the extra iCare package that you and Susanna sent last week. I hope someday to pay you back for all of this. I pray for you every day.

Aimee taught me that we put the hand of the hurting into the hand of the Savior when we walk the Emmaus road with them. And that is the heart of the gospel.

Aimee's situation reminds me of Psalm 147:2–4:

> The Lord builds up Jerusalem;
> > he gathers the outcasts of Israel.
> He heals the brokenhearted
> > and binds up their wounds.

> He determines the number of the stars;
> he gives to all of them their names.

The God who names and numbers the stars holds in his scarred hands the shards of your broken heart. Of this I am sure.

The Bible offers good and realistic and powerful answers, but answers fall short without the pierced hands and feet of Jesus. Ordinary hospitality is the hands and feet of Jesus, and it holds people together with letters to prison or hugs. Hospitality reaches across worldview to be the bridge of gospel grace. Jesus did not come with self-defense. He came with bread. He came with fish. So too must we.

Just before Aimee was moved from the county jail to begin her prison sentence in Georgia, she was baptized. She described what it was like to emerge from the water to see her hands bound in chains and cuffs, the Carolina blue sky a backdrop of hope beyond the chains. I suspect that she understood something about Jesus in the backdrop of chains and cuffs that I am still too dumb to appreciate.

Conclusion:
Feeding the Five Thousand

The Nuts and Bolts and Beans and Rice

Radically ordinary hospitality sees our Christian homes as hospitals and incubators. We gather in the spiritually poor, crippled, blind, and broken because we have been there—and not so long ago. We know the contours and seductions of our former atheism. We are capable of any and all evil, and we know that. Our choice temptations still know our names and addresses. We are weak. We come to Christ with nothing—we bring nothing useful for our own salvation. We are rendered lame by sin. We are unable to see God's truth on our own terms. We need God to come to us, to rescue us, because we can't summon the strength to save ourselves, and, even if we could, we would not know where to go. And this is what Jesus Christ did and does. Through union with and growth in Christ, we are made new. We are redeemed, forgiven, and embraced as adopted children of God. We are called to die to ourselves and our choice sins, even those that have been our kind company for as long as we can remember. We are called to repent of the original sin that distorts us, the actual sin that distracts us, and the indwelling sin that manipulates us. This is a high and hard calling. We are given supernatural power to love the things God loves and to eschew those things he hates. We do not barter with the Bible on these matters. And as we walk with Christ, he renews us and restores so that we have plenty to give to others.

Christians are not fearful hoarders; we are fearless givers. Psalm 112 tells us why:

> The righteous will never be moved;
>> he will be remembered forever.
> He is not afraid of bad news;
>> his heart is firm, trusting in the LORD. (vv. 6–7)

Or, as the New Living Translation renders it: "They do not fear bad news; they confidently trust the LORD to care for them." Radically ordinary hospitality manifests confident trust that the Lord will care for us and that he will care for others through our obedience.

But how does God multiply the fishes and the loaves? How does he feed the five thousand? How does he use us?

All Christians are called to practice hospitality in their homes. Households run by single Christians are just as vital, necessary, and needed in the practice of hospitality as those run by married people. Households without children and households with children each model Christ's blessings. The redeemed rich and the redeemed poor and everyone in between are called to practice Christian hospitality in households, dorm rooms, bus stops, and community gardens.

Boundaries

In married households it is vital that both husband and wife share a calling for hospitality and work together to establish a budget for time and food and people. Wives, let your husband lead. Husbands, be sensitive to your wife's energy level. Kent and I use the marathon training model. The key to running a marathon is to value a slow and steady pace. When two people train for a marathon together, the slowest runner sets the pace. The same is true for husband-wife team hospitality: the pace is set by the one who feels the most frail. Kent and I have been a hospitality team for over a decade now, and we see each other's distinct gifts and boundaries. But hospitality should never divide a family; it should make us stronger in Christ. If hospitality becomes a point of contention, something is wrong. Stop and reevaluate. Pray. Map out goals and values. Be a team.

Schedules

I love beans and rice.

Jasmine rice or short, brown rice. Either works. Rice is the most perfect grain. Black beans bubbling gently with a little cumin and red pepper and salt and olive oil and garlic. Lately I have been serving Indian dhal made with red lentils, ginger, curry, garam masala, and red pepper. So many people around here like to eat this, so I make it every day. We call it the Daily Dhal. You might also find in my kitchen an organic chicken in the Crock-Pot, plugged in the corner, cooking slowly on low. The nuts and bolts of our hospitality ministry are beans, rice, vegetables, and sometimes chicken.

There is nothing glamorous about daily hospitality. It is not showy or fancy. But it helps that before I walk the dogs in the morning, the basics for our daily meals are in the ready. Table fellowship is central to our daily work, and good food matters. But other things are more pressing priorities: homeschooling Knox and Mary and serving my church family and neighbors and writing this book. So, if by 6:45 a.m.—the time that I usually walk the dogs—rice is steaming, beans are simmering, and chicken is slow-cooking, then at least I know I have the basics covered to feed people as they come.

The tools for daily table fellowship are set in habit for me. But most other things require schedules, written on a spiral notebook that stays in the kitchen. This schedule reminds us that we need to vacuum our house and wipe down the bathrooms daily. (Deep cleanings happen every other week.) It also includes other chore lists and the weekly shopping lists. People who live with us and people who are stakeholders in our hospitality ministry often add to the list or offer to pick up things listed or take over specific tasks. Radically ordinary Christian hospitality is a community effort.

I keep homeschool schedules separate, but I also use spiral notebooks for these, one per child. I find schedules—especially the paper kind that are accessible to others and daily revised—crucial.

Our home is a beautiful, messy blessing to us. We use it for many, many things. It is where we work and where we care for people. Our large mahogany dining room table is fifty-four inches across the middle and long enough to seat twenty-five. Aside from holidays, it stays open to its midsize length—the one that allows us to pull fifteen chairs around it. This table has been in Kent's family for five generations, and it has been the setting for more gospel conversations than I can record. If only it could talk. I love our table. I try to take good care of it.

A Day in the Life

I prepare for daily hospitality in our home and at our table. If for some odd reason, we are the only ones there, then I have food to freeze. No big problem. In regular and daily ways, by dinnertime, our house is usually filled with a friend or two from church, a friend or two from the neighborhood, and a group of children. We have gathered together enough times that as new people join us, we can all make them feel welcome.

In our house, and in the Bible, people take on the roles and responsibilities of both host and guest. Our routine of daily hospitality means that my children have plenty of examples of Christian living—including the important example set by vital, vibrant, Christian adults who are single. Our routine means that our children watch adults they respect struggle with big issues before the Lord. This makes their own personal struggles less frightening. In our house it is normal to struggle with sin and to do so openly. Repentance is a Christian fruit, not a social shame.

Last year when I was Christmas caroling with Donna and a group from the neighborhood, I received a text message from my friend Aileen. She had just found out that another neighbor had been diagnosed with cancer, and Aileen and her family were stricken by the injustice of it. The sick one was the single dad of a special-needs child. Why would God do this? Between "Deck the Halls" and "Silent Night," I invited Aileen's family over for dinner that night. We then made a dining table from every flat surface, as we were also hosting a missionary family. Aileen brought over an extra pot of soup, which was wonderful.

After dinner and Bible reading, one neighbor said, "I find myself in a room full of theologians." Then, turning to Kent and the missionaries, he went on: "Why did God do this to Kevin? Why did he allow him to have incurable cancer when he is so needed by his daughter?"

Such good and vital questions. Such a good and vital time and place to ask such questions. Kent and others opened their Bibles and their hearts. One missionary friend, Michael, said something that affected the children powerfully: "The best time to learn the mystery of God's providence is before the crisis hits. The time is now for all of us to know God as our Creator and Savior."

We gathered twenty people around two tables and prayed for our newly diagnosed neighbor. And then we set up a rotation to provide him with meals. After dinner the children played Monopoly and Connect Four, and the adults talked some more about illness and eternity and God's mercy.

And when another day was done, and we counted our blessings, we marveled at how God had graciously used our table to host and to heal, to guest and to give. How did we know that a family would receive crisis information and need to talk through it? We didn't. But when crisis hit, they knew that they could ask us. They knew that they could come. They knew that it was no trouble. They knew that in our house we talk about anything, and then we go to the throne of grace with all our fears and doubts and pain. And how did they know? A hospitality house speaks for itself. Look at all the cars parked outside. Look at the lights on. Look at the kids playing on the tire swing. Look at the neighbors already gathering. Look at the open door. It's here for all to see.

We take time to prepare our home and our hearts for daily hospitality. It is intentional and well rehearsed. But we also know that there are many common barriers to daily hospitality. Certainly there are unavoidable, legitimate barriers, but so often the barriers are a false sense of entitlement based on gifts and interests, the danger of bad habits and hidden sin, counterfeit hospitality, and the idols of achievement and acquisition. Daily, we fight these sins that stand as barriers to hospitality.

False Sense of Entitlement Based on Gifts and Interests

My Myers-Briggs score is INTJ. I also have a light-sensitivity issue that has grown worse during the last five years, as public speaking puts me under stage lights. I am a classic introvert. This means that I draw an inner charge and refueling from being alone, preferably with a book, a cat, and some knitting. I know how to engage people, but being with people is draining. Therefore, I get up earlier than everyone else in my house, because I need my alone time. I putter in the kitchen, I read my Bible, I write my books, I fold laundry. And I renew my energy and focus by spending my alone time well.

We introverts miss out on great blessings when we excuse ourselves from practicing hospitality because it exhausts us. I often find people exhausting. But over the years I have learned how to pace myself, how to prepare for the private time necessary to recharge, and how to grow in discomfort. Knowing your personality and your sensitivities does not excuse you from ministry. It means that you need to prepare for it differently than others might.

The Danger of Bad Habits and Hidden Sin

We all come to Christ with bad habits. We are all called to learn new ones and to unlearn others (Eph. 4:22–24). Bad habits are hard to discern and harder still to abandon.

Have you taken the time to unlearn bad habits? Or have you surrounded yourself with people who enable your bad habits, all in the delusion that your giftedness entitles you to them? My gifts (and yours) are, at best, filthy rags (Isa. 64:6). God calls us to serve and give and not to get credit for either.

Sometimes it is hard to identify bad habits that are hidden by personality or history. The best way to start knowing yourself is to ask others who know you well to help you see yourself more clearly. Ask your elders and people close to you to help you identify those sins of selfish ambition that may be hidden to you. Ask. And then kill sin. Don't excuse it. Don't make false peace with it. Die to self. Grow in Christ.

Counterfeit Hospitality

We live in a world awash in counterfeit hospitality. Knowing the difference between the grace of God and its counterfeit is crucial to Christian living.

Something is counterfeit when it imitates with the intent to deceive. A counterfeit dollar imitates the real deal, and it hopes you will buy in to the falsehood.

Counterfeit hospitality is sometimes dangerous and sinister, like sex trafficking and pornography, both of which promise intimacy, deliver enslavement, and create a culture of unimaginable abuse, violence, inhumanity, and injustice for the (mostly) women and children who are horrifically chained to such a life. Sex trafficking is linked to pornography. When a church identifies a sin pattern of its people (such as pornography), it also has a responsibility to protect the victims created by that sin. Repentance calls for nothing short of this. Counterfeit hospitality demands a kind of compartmentalized mental surgery and excuse-making for sin patterns. The gospel is cosmological and holistic. It takes no prisoners. Jesus died for it all, and when he rose again, he came with the power to live differently, to live sacrificially.

Counterfeit hospitality can sometimes seem benign. The barista at Starbucks engages in counterfeit hospitality, but that is not sinful. The use of your extra bedroom for Airbnb is also counterfeit hospitality, and that too is not sinful. There is nothing necessarily wrong with being a barista at Starbucks or using your spare room for Air B&B. But there is something wrong with thinking that you are practicing hospitality as you get paid for these services.

If you believe that counterfeit hospitality exempts you from the real deal, then you start to see things in a skewed way. Counterfeit hospitality separates host and guest in ways that allow no blending of the two roles. Such separation should be the first red flag. Counterfeit hospitality creates false divisions and false binaries: noble givers or needy receivers. Or hired givers and privileged receivers. Benefactors and beneficiaries are both tainted under counterfeit hospitality. Counterfeit hospitality comes with strings; Christian hospitality comes with strangers becoming neighbors becoming family of God and gathering in the great expectation of God's coming world.

One reason that too many Christians fail to practice ordinary, radical, Christian hospitality is that we have become so duped and distracted by its counterfeit that we don't know what we need.

The Idols of Achievement and Acquisition

One kind of household is absolutely incompetent at the practice of hospitality—utterly and completely incapable. It is as useless as grasping at the wind. The household that loves things too much and loves people too little cannot honor God through the practice of radically ordinary hospitality. The household that has too much and thinks too highly of material possessions has become seduced by the idols of acquisition and achievement. If you love acquisition and achievement, you will never practice hospitality. You might have like-minded people who come and bow before your idols, but you won't ever practice hospitality. If the white carpet is an idol—or the new paint or the couch or your private liquor collection or your semi-pornographic videos or any other vile, soulless thing—you are too sinful to do the most basic Christian practice: open your home in real time.

Sometimes Christians tell me that they don't practice hospitality because they don't have enough space, dishes, or food. They fear that they do not have enough to give. This is a false fear that no one should heed. Hospitality shares what there is; that's all. It's not entertainment. It's not supposed to be.

In reality, Christians who have too much are the ones prohibited from practicing hospitality. They have so many cluttered idols that they can give nothing at all. For this reason, it is often the well-heeled and rich who are known for their lack of hospitality, and the meager and even poor who are known for their plentiful hospitality. So, Christian, kill your idols. First John 2:15–17 tells us how:

> Do not love the world or the things in the world. If anyone loves the world, the love of the Father is not in him. For all that is in the world—the desires of the flesh and the desires of the eyes and pride of life—is not from the Father but is from the world. And the world is passing away along with its desires, but whoever does the will of God abides forever.

Many years ago, a family in our church developed what they believed was a holy hatred of our hospitality ministry. When we gave away our van to an international seminary student and his family for the academic school year, this family was vocal and critical. Truth be told, if we had a bigger church, one where the diaconal fund could help in such ways, then the pastor would not need to give up the second car. But Kent and I were happy to cut back and to sacrifice. And our neighbors Kristin and Ryan were just around the corner to help when we needed rides. It was good to ask for help when we needed it and to give up something valuable to help another family. We believe that sacrifice prepares us for ministry in important ways, so we handed over the keys. Slowly, word of the gift leaked out, and it became clear that the family who was critical of us felt that there was something wrong with the way we practiced hospitality. They thought it ostentatious. Too much. They were doing a slow burn about it.

Once after church, my son and one of the children in this family were talking about Thanksgiving.

"Who came over to your house?" my son asked.

The boy said, "Two chairs and no more!"

Confused, my son asked for an explanation. The boy said that their family motto was "Family first, so two chairs and no more!" What did he mean? He meant that the family patriarch intentionally kept only two extra dining-room chairs in their large palatial home so that they could never have more than two guests at a time. It ensured that they had family time.

My son asked, "Which two people did you have over?"

The other boy replied, "No one. It was just us. Kind of boring."

As my son was recounting this strange exchange at dinner that night, he shared that he still did not understand why "two chairs and no more" would actually stand in the way of having Thanksgiving guests. Knox is exceedingly literal in his interpretation of things, and he didn't make the leap that in some houses, if people cannot sit in chairs, they cannot come in. In our house, chairs are not an obstacle. People have taken Thanksgiving dinner plates to the grass, to the trampoline, to the neon-green picnic table, to the porch, and, routinely, to the coffee table and the floor.

The "two chairs and no more" family were not mean-spirited people. But their idols left no room for hospitality. They simply had too much. And people who have too much often take themselves too seriously to actually give themselves to others in the way that God's hospitality commands require.

What If?

Imagine a world where every Christian practiced radically ordinary hospitality as either host or guest.

Imagine a world where every Christian made a covenant of church membership and honored it.

Imagine a world where every Christian tithed, and where we lived intentionally below our means, having enough to share and moving into neighborhoods that need us more often than we need them.

Imagine a world where living as image bearers of a holy God meant something, something that changed the way we saw ourselves and others.

Imagine a world where neighbors said that Christians throw the best parties in town and are the go-to people for big problems and issues, without being invited.

Imagine if the children in the neighborhood knew that the Christians were safe people to ask for help when unthinkable agony canvassed their private or family lives.

Imagine a world where men lived as men of God and women lived as women of God, and children—including those not yet born—were valued as children of God. One where gender and sexuality roles were known to be blessings to others, even when they required great sacrifice. One where being born male or female comes with distinct blessings and constraints, and where our roles as men and women were valued as high and distinctive callings.

Imagine a world where every Christian knew his neighbors sufficiently to be of earthly and spiritual good.

Imagine a world where every Christian knew by name people who lived in poverty or prison, felt tied to them and to their futures, and lived differently because of it.

Imagine a world where sexuality was safe within the confines of biblical boundaries and was not unleashed in rape, incest, pornography, and self-harm.

Imagine a world where *biblical* patriarchy—the benevolent leading of servant-hearted fathers—made all of us breathe a sigh of relief, knowing that the good fathers would protect us from the roving gangs of evil men.

Imagine a world where the fruit of repentance and the practice of hospitality mark the reputations of Christians for those who do not yet believe that Jesus saves by the very same power that raised him from the grave.

Imagine a world where people take back the night in prayer.

Imagine a world where you know the names of your neighbors, and you play cards with them and eat meals together, praying for the children in the neighborhood and lending a helping hand before you are asked.

Imagine a world where no one languishes in crushing

loneliness, where no abused woman or man or child suffers alone, where people take their real and pressing problems to Christians who have the reputation of being helpers, and where victims are not swept away, lost, forgotten.

Imagine a world where people fear God more than men and serve God more than comfort.

Imagine a world where the power of the gospel to change lives is ours to behold.

This is the world that the Bible imagines for us. That is the world that Jesus prays for us to create in his name. Not because any of this—tithing, church membership, hospitality, advocating for victims—is heaven on earth. It is not. Rather, we do these things so that we can prepare, arm in arm, for what is coming next, for the return of Christ, for our inheritance in the new heavens and the new earth, so that we can warn our neighbors of the real judgment to come, so that we can honor our God and King.

That is the nuts and bolts of it, yes? Starting with you and me and our open door and our dinner table and our house key poised for the giving. This is not complex. Radically ordinary, daily Christianity is not PhD Christianity. The gospel coming with a house key is ABC Christianity. Radically ordinary and daily hospitality is the basic building block for vital Christian living. Start anywhere. But do start.

Acknowledgments

Now to him who is able to keep you from stumbling and to present you blameless before the presence of his glory with great joy, to the only God, our Savior, through Jesus Christ our Lord, be glory, majesty, dominion, and authority, before all time and now and forever. Amen. —Jude 24–25

As a pastor, my husband, Kent, blesses the congregation with a benediction each Lord's Day. He has used other benedictions throughout our sixteen years of marriage, but Jude 24–25 is my favorite. These words lift me. These words launch me. How thankful I am that my Lord Jesus Christ keeps me from stumbling, and how thankful I am for the brothers and sisters who have kept me from stumbling or caught me in midair during the writing of this book.

I am thankful to Kent for his love, fortitude, unwavering faith, compassion, and commitment to hospitality. God radically converted both of us. Without anything close to a family history of Christianity, we both remember the odd incongruity of being newly converted and harrowingly lonely. Kent's belief that Christian hospitality and its kingdom-building vitality are more important than personal achievement or acquisition is indelibly inscribed on every page of this book.

The encouragement of our children refuels me daily. Watching Knox and Mary grow, make professions of faith in Christ, serve the church and the community, and face down challenges of learning and life has inspired me to be a better servant of Christ. The writing and editing of this book was daily punctuated by rescued (or kidnapped) turtles, the lost and found dogs (ours and others', but somehow always managing to acquire more than we started with), and amphibians and reptiles mysteriously arriving in the home-school room (or worse, my bedroom) in various life stages (including impossible-to-separate mating toads that became part of a skip-counting math game, but don't tell PETA). That life is messy and delightful all at once is my daily reality because of you two.

Beholding Michael, our oldest son who was adopted at the age of seventeen, excel in his job, take care of his wife, and love and protect his baby is a joy to behold. I'm so glad that you live close to us, and I am delighted to have been made a grandmother this year. I love you, dear ones, and I thank God that he allowed me to be your mom.

My friends, many of whom lived through the awkward encounters captured here—thank you, and I love you: Bob and Donna Mutter, Hope and Will Roberts, Susanna Stevens, and Ryan and Kristin Stults. Donna, this book would not have been written without your faithful tutoring of my children. Hope, your organization of a Christ-loyal team of praying sisters and brothers—and you, dear and beloved praying sisters and brothers!—shook the gates of eternity for the many people I have had the honor to hold and hug and hear from as I speak and travel. If you had a nickel for every meal you made for me or special Juice Plus delivery, you would be a rich woman. Susanna, your willingness to read drafts of this book and give me forthright feedback, travel with me to speaking events, be my friend in spite of my many failings, and pick up Chipotle dinners when I'm torn between writing books and cooking for the masses have saved me on more occasions than I can count. Kristin, I so depend on your can-do spirit, your vulnerability and transparency, and your sincere desire to grow to be more like Christ. It is my honor to homeschool together with you and to be in each other's daily lives. Having children who love and support one another as much as we do is so inspiring! Thank you all for the countless nights that end with prayer together.

To friends afar, but not far at all because of prayer: Dr. David Noe, thank you for your friendship throughout these years and for Latinperdiem.com—which is every homeschool mom's favorite Latin inoculation in the morning. (If you, my readers, haven't heard of this, you are in for a wonderful surprise.) To M. K., my dear son in the Lord, thank you for reading this manuscript and helping me to put others before myself in my prose. To Pastor Ken Smith, thank you for your faithful ministry to me, for your daily prayers for my protection and usefulness to the Lord, and for your continued good advice and counsel. Thank you for being my father in the Lord. To Drew and Lynne Gordon, thank you for these many fruitful and challenging years of ministry together, thrust as we were to the front lines of a vital public conversation about gospel faith and biblical sexuality, and for first taking the chance on publishing me.

To my church family at First Reformed Presbyterian Church of Durham, thank you for loving hospitality as much as God does.

To Christopher Yuan, thank you for your daily prayers, much needed (and often daily) good and godly advice, generous and joyful life of faith in Christ and service to God, and being my witty brother in the Lord. Our testimonies make me know that I am not alone in this world.

To Sam Allberry, thank you for believing with me that the blood of Christ is thicker than the blood of biology.

To professionals who took care of me and this book from start to finish: Robert Wolgemuth and Austin Wilson, you are loyal and lionhearted agents, and you ably took care of all the details that make for a fluent pen. Justin Taylor, you have been to me an incorruptible and stalwart editor, looking out for me and for this book from start to finish. Thank you. Lydia Brownback, I thank God for your prescient vision of how this book might be used to serve God and his people, for the wise and strong books that you have written, and for helping me delve deeply into the art and beauty of writing, a craft that we both love so deeply. Fellow morning person, it was wonderful to work with you in the dark of the morning, knowing that a 4:30 a.m. email was going to a fellow coffee-drinking, Bible-reading sister.

To my neighbors, thank you for being scrappy and loving and fun and present and for walking with me these many years (usually with our dogs and children in tow) as we seek to build community together. Your names have been changed (unless you gave me permission to use the real ones!), and many of our anecdotes condensed (as daily hospitality means that I had more anecdotes than pages!). Please forgive me if I omitted something that you wanted to see in here. You are loved and valued. Doing life with you is pure joy.

Finally, I am thankful to my Lord, for his alien righteousness imputed to me, for his galvanizing power to make and remake, to forgive and reconcile, to restore, to launch into the world in his name; and for the Bible, my ontology, my guide to faith and life, my lifeblood. Only God's love is seamless. Living in and for Christ does not require compartmentalization or mental surgery, scapegoating or manipulating of people, ideas, histories, or identities. Living in and for Christ is comprehensive, coherent, hopeful, and seamless, and reaches into eternity. If what I am writing here is new, please take my hand and feel the hand of the Savior beckoning you to reconciliation and peace in eternity with him. This is real. This is true. Nothing is more important than this.

Notes

Chapter 1: Priceless

1. The names of many friends who appear on these pages have been changed for the protection of personal privacy.

Chapter 2: The Jesus Paradox

1. Susan Hunt has a lovely devotional on this in the *Women's Devotional Bible* (Wheaton, IL: Crossway, 2014): "From Empty to Full," 1269.
2. Ibid.
3. *Habitus* is a favorite word concept of mine. I take my definition here from Pierre Bourdieu, *Distinction: A Social Critique of the Judgement of Taste* (London: Routledge University Press, 1984).
4. Mary Douglas, *Implicit Meanings: Selected Essays in Anthropology*, 2nd ed. (London: Routlege University Press, 1999), 231–52.
5. Alain Badiou, Pierre Bourdieu, et al., *What Is a People? New Directions in Critical Theory*, trans. Jody Gladding (New York: Columbia University Press, 2016), 9.
6. Russell Moore, *Onward: Engaging the Culture without Losing the Gospel* (Nashville, TN: B&H, 2015), 227.

Chapter 3: Our Post-Christian World

1. "The Promise Keepers' Message Is a Threat to Democracy," April 15, 1997. See also Anne M. Stiles, "Prof. Decries Promise Keepers: Syracuse Professor Speaks at the Barker Center about Her Upcoming Book," *The Harvard Crimson*, October 24, 1997.
2. Theo Hobson, *Reinventing Liberal Christianity* (Grand Rapids, MI: Eerdmans, 2013).
3. Tim Challies, "Marks of a Moral Revolution," Challies.com, accessed May 8, 2017, https://www.challies.com/final-call/final-call-january-17/.
4. For an introduction to the history of sexual orientation, please see Rosaria Champagne Butterfield, *Openness Unhindered: Further Thoughts of an Unlikely Convert on Sexuality and Union with Christ* (Pittsburgh, PA: Crown & Covenant, 2015), 93–112.

5. John Calvin, *365 Days with John Calvin: A Collection of Daily Readings from the Writings of John Calvin*, ed. Joel Beeke (Grand Rapids, MI: Reformation Heritage, 2008), May 9 entry.

6. Red-letter Christians are those who use selected words of Jesus, which are often highlighted in the red-letter editions of some Bibles, to bear on social issues.

7. David Gushee, "Christians, Conflict, and Change," *Religion News Service*, accessed May 9, 2017, http://religionnews.com/columns/david-gushee/.

8. For an accessible introduction to the doctrine of union with Christ, see Rankin Wilbourne, *Union with Christ: The Way to Know and Enjoy God* (Colorado Springs, CO: David C. Cook, 2016). For a specific understanding of the three distinctive forms of union with Christ, see Joel R. Beeke and Mark Jones, *A Puritan Theology: Doctrine for Life* (Grand Rapids, MI: Reformation Heritage, 2012), 482. Theologians also use other words to describe this threefold union: (1) *predestinarian*; (2) *redemptive-historical*; and (3) *existential*. The words may differ, but the ideas are the same.

9. Gloria Furman, *Missional Motherhood: The Everyday Ministry of Motherhood in the Grand Plan of God* (Wheaton, IL: Crossway, 2016).

Chapter 4: God Never Gets the Address Wrong

1. Wesley Hill, "If the Church Were a Haven," *First Things*, Institute of Religion and Public Life, June 27, 2016, accessed August 1, 2017, https://www-firstthings.com/web-exclusives/2016/06-if-the-church-were-a-haven.

2. Dictionary.com, s.v. "symposium," accessed April 11, 2017, http://www.dictionary.com/browse/symposium?s=t.

3. Tim Chester, *A Meal with Jesus: Discovering Grace, Community, and Mission around the Table* (Wheaton, IL: Crossway, 2011), 38–39.

4. *KJV Study Bible*, ed. Joel Beeke (Grand Rapids, MI: Reformation Heritage, 2014), Luke 7:50 note.

5. Johannes Geerhardus Vos, *The Westminster Larger Catechism: A Commentary*, ed. G. I. Williamson (Phillipsburg, NJ: P&R, 2002), 53. Question 21: "Did man continue in that estate wherein God at first created him?" Answer: "Our first parents, being left to the freedom of their own will, through the temptation of Satan, transgressed the commandment of God in eating the forbidden fruit; and thereby fell from the estate of innocency wherein they were created."

Chapter 5: The Gospel Comes with a House Key

1. The very best book to read about the AIDS crisis and how it brought together the LGBTQ community is David France, *How to Survive a Plague: The Inside Story of How Citizens and Science Tamed AIDS* (New York: Alfred Knopf, 2016).

2. Westminster Confession of Faith, chap. 7.

3. http://safe-families.org/.

4. The very best book for men to learn and understand the role of husband as shepherd is Robert Wolgemuth, *Like the Shepherd: Leading Your Marriage with Love and Grace* (Washington, DC: Regency Faith, 2017).
5. Christopher Yuan and Angela Yuan, *Out of a Far Country: A Gay Son's Journey to God; a Broken Mother's Search for Hope* (Colorado Springs, CO: Waterbrook, 2011).
6. Dietrich Bonhoeffer, *Life Together: A Discussion of Christian Fellowship*, trans. John W. Doberstein (New York: Harper & Row, 1954), 112.
7. http://safe-families.org/.
8. Viet Thanh Nguyen, "Points of No Return: Book Review of *Exit West*, by Mohsin Hamid," *New York Times* book review (March 12, 2017), 1.
9. Marit Newton, "Mass Migration," *2016 Personal Prayer Diary* (Seattle: YWAM, 2016), 20–21. Also see Thomas Albinson, "A Christian Response to the Humanitarian Crisis in the Mediterranean," *Christian Post* (April 26, 2015), accessed July 13, 2017, http://www.christianpost.com/news/a-christian-response-to-the-humanitiarian-crisis-in-the-mediterranean-138151/.
10. An excellent resource on the worldwide refugee crisis is Stephan Bauman, Matthew Soerens, and Issam Smeir, *Seeking Refuge: On the Shores of the Global Refugee Crisis* (Chicago: Moody, 2016).

Chapter 6: Judas in the Church
1. *Restoring the Soul of a Church: Healing Congregations Wounded by Clergy Sexual Misconduct*, ed. Nancy Myer Hopkins and Mark Laaser (Collegeville, MN: Liturgical Press, 1995).
2. F. W. Krummacher, *The Suffering Saviour: A Series of Devotional Meditations* (1856, repr. Carlisle, PA: Banner of Truth, 2004), 61.
3. Matthew Henry, *Complete Commentary*, accessed August 2, 2017, http://www.biblestudytools.com/commentaries/matthew-henry-complete/matthew/26.html.
4. Alfred Edersheim writes, "The sum spent was very large, remembering that 200 dinars (about 6 pounds) nearly sufficed to provide bread for 5,000 men with their families, and that the ordinary wage of a laborer amounted by only one dinar a day." *The Life and Times of Jesus the Messiah* (Peabody, MA: Hendrickson, 1993), 721.
5. Ibid.
6. Ibid., 722.
7. Krummacher, *Suffering Saviour*, 62.
8. Ibid., 63.
9. Ibid., 64.
10. Ibid., 67.
11. Ibid., 68–69.

Chapter 7: Giving up the Ghosts
1. https://www.bobsflakes.com/.

2. "Psalm 23D," *The Book of Psalms for Worship* (Pittsburgh, PA: Crown & Covenant, 2011).
3. Ibid.
4. Ibid.

Chapter 8: The Daily Grind
1. For more information, visit http://songsforsaplings.com/.
2. Jen Wilkin, *Women of the Word: How to Study the Bible with Both Our Hearts and Our Minds* (Wheaton, IL: Crossway, 2014).
3. Rosaria Champagne Butterfield, *The Secret Thoughts of an Unlikely Convert: An English Professor's Journey into Christian Faith* (Pittsburgh, PA: Crown & Covenant, 2012).

Chapter 9: Blessed Are the Merciful
1. Crown & Covenant, *Refuge: Selections from the Book of Psalms for Worship* (Syracuse, NY: Syracuse RPC, n.d.).
2. David France, *How to Survive a Plague: The Inside Story of How Citizens and Science Tamed AIDS* (New York: Alfred Knopf, 2016), 48.

Chapter 10: Walking the Emmaus Road
1. Matthew Henry, *Matthew Henry's Concise Commentary on the Whole Bible* (Nashville, TN: Thomas Nelson, 1997), 976–77.
2. Ibid., 976.

Recommended Reading

Allberry, Sam. *Why Bother with Church?: And Other Questions about Why You Need It and Why It Needs You*. Surrey, UK: Good Book Company, 2016.

Bauman, Stephan, Matthew Soerens, and Issam Smeir. *Seeking Refuge: On the Shores of the Global Refugee Crisis*. Chicago: Moody, 2016.

Bence, Evelyn. *Room at My Table: Preparing Heart and Home for Christian Hospitality*. Nashville, TN: Upper Room Books, 2014.

Blomberg, Craig L. *Contagious Holiness: Jesus' Meals with Sinners*. New Studies in Biblical Theology. Downers Grove, IL: InterVarsity Press, 2005.

Calvin, John. *A Little Book on the Christian Life*. Reprint, Orlando, FL: Reformation Trust, 2017.

Chester, Tim. *A Meal with Jesus: Discovering Grace, Community, and Mission around the Table*. Wheaton, IL: Crossway, 2011.

Clark, Marion, ed. *The Problem of Good: When the World Seems Fine without God*. Phillipsburg, NJ: P&R, 2014.

Clarkson, Sally, and Sarah Clarkson. *The Life-Giving Home: Creating a Place of Belonging and Becoming*. Carol Stream, IL: Tyndale, 2016.

Clements, Brandon, and Dustin Willis. *The Simplest Way to Change the World: Biblical Hospitality as a Way of Life*. Chicago: Moody, 2016.

Douglas, Mary. *Implicit Meanings: Selected Essays in Anthropology*. 2nd ed. London: Routledge Press, 1999.

————. *Purity and Danger: An Analysis of the Concepts of Pollution and Taboo*. London: Routledge Press, 1966. Reprint, 1996.

Ehman, Karen. *A Life That Says Welcome: Simple Ways to Open Your Heart and Home to Others*. Grand Rapids, MI: Revell, 2006.

Ennis, Pat, and Lisa Tatlock. *Practicing Hospitality: The Joy of Serving Others*. Wheaton, IL: Crossway, 2007.

France, David. *How to Survive a Plague: The Inside Story of How Citizens and Science Tamed AIDS*. New York: Alfred Knopf, 2016.

Furman, Gloria. *Missional Motherhood: The Everyday Ministry of Motherhood in the Grand Plan of God*. Wheaton, IL: Crossway, 2016.

Hellerman, Joseph H. *When the Church Was a Family: Recapturing Jesus' Vision for Authentic Christian Community*. Nashville, TN: B&H, 2009.

Mains, Karen. *Open Heart, Open Home: The Hospitable Way to Make Others Feel Welcome and Wanted*. Downers Grove, IL: InterVarsity Press, 1976.

Moore, Russell. *Onward: Engaging the Culture without Losing the Gospel*. Nashville, TN: B&H, 2015.

Nichols, Stephen J. *A Time for Confidence: Trusting God in a Post-Christian Society*. Orlando, FL: Reformation Trust, 2016.

Niequist, Shauna. *Bread and Wine: A Love Letter to Life around the Table with Recipes*. Grand Rapids, MI: Zondervan, 2013.

Nouwen, Henri J. M. *Reaching Out: The Three Movements of the Spiritual Life*. New York: Doubleday, 1975.

Oden, Amy G. *God's Welcome: Hospitality for a Gospel-Hungry World*. Cleveland, OH: Pilgrim Press, 2008.

Palmer, Parker J. *The Company of Strangers: Christians and the Renewal of America's Public Life*. New York: Crossroad, 1981.

Pathak, Jay, and Dave Runyon. *The Art of Neighboring: Building Genuine Relationships Right Outside Your Door*. Grand Rapids, MI: Baker, 2012.

Pohl, Christine D. *Living into Community: Cultivating Practices That Sustain Us*. Grand Rapids, MI: Eerdmans, 2012.

————. *Making Room: Recovering Hospitality as a Christian Tradition*. Grand Rapids, MI: Eerdmans, 1999.

Schaeffer, Edith. *L'Abri*. Wheaton, IL: Crossway, 1992.

Sicks, Christopher. *Tangible: Making God Known through Deeds of Mercy and Words of Truth.* Colorado Springs, CO: NavPress, 2013.

Strauch, Alexander. *The Hospitality Commands.* Littleton, CO: Lewis & Roth, 1993.

Sutherland, Arthur. *I Was a Stranger: A Christian Theology of Hospitality.* Nashville, TN: Abingdon Press, 2006.

Ten Boom, Corrie. *The Hiding Place.* Grand Rapids, MI: Chosen Press, 1971. Reprint, 2006.

Vos, Johannes G. *The Westminster Larger Catechism: A Commentary.* Edited by G. I. Williamson. Phillipsburg, NJ: P&R, 2002.

Wilbourne, Rankin. *Union with Christ: The Way to Know and Enjoy God.* Colorado Springs, CO: David C. Cook, 2016.

Wilken, Robert Louis. *The Christians as the Romans Saw Them.* 2nd ed. New Haven, CT: Yale University Press, 2003.

Williamson, G. I., ed. *The Westminster Confession of Faith for Study Classes.* Phillipsburg, NJ: P&R, 2004.

Willis, Dustin. *Life in Community: Joining Together to Display the Gospel.* Chicago: Moody, 2015.

Wolgemuth, Robert. *Like the Shepherd: Leading Your Marriage with Love and Grace.* Washington, DC: Regnery Faith, 2017.

General Index

God, 197; authority of, 32; love of, 87; mercy of, 87; perseverance of, 56; providence of, 56
goodness, distinction of from holiness, 54–56
Gordon, Drew, 169–70, 171–72, 204
Gordon, Lynne, 169–70, 171–72, 204
gospel, the, and a house key, 95–98, 99, 116, 220
grace, 58, 100, 116, 200–201; common grace, 55; contagious grace, 29–31, 117; irresistible grace, 56; special grace, 55–56
Graham, Billy, 169
Grandin, Temple, 191
Gushee, David, 57

habits, bad, 214
habitus, 33, 64, 94, 225n3
Henry, Matthew, 135–36, 201
Hill, Wesley, "If the Church Were a Haven," 70
Hobson, Theo, *Reinventing Liberal Christianity*, 51
holiness, distinction of from goodness, 54–56
Holy Spirit, 29, 59, 61, 87–88
home, the: as hospital and incubator, 64, 93–98, 209; short-term and dependable hospitality in, 101–7
hospitality, counterfeit, 70, 71, 215–16; as benign, 215–16; as dangerous and sinister, 215 (*see* gay clubs; pornography; sex trafficking); and the intent to deceive, 215; and separation of host and guest, 216
hospitality, deathbed, 154–55
hospitality, radically ordinary, 30, 31–36, 36–37, 209–10; and the authority of God and church, 32; and boundaries, 33, 127, 210–11; and budgeting, 63; and caring about the things

that neighbors care about, 161–66; and children, 108–9, 116, 172–77; as a community effort, 211; difference from social-gospel practices, 32; and hosts and guests, 37; as image-bearer driven, 64; and knowledge of who our neighbors are and how they struggle, 32; and living as living epistles, 109–12; and looking out for old people, 168–69; the meaning of *ordinary*, 36; the meaning of *radical*, 36; the practice of radically ordinary hospitality as good for the giver, 116–17; and the principle of tithing, 37; purpose of, 31, 34; and relocation to neighborhoods hit hard by drugs, crime, and poverty, 169–71; and schedules, 211–12; solving the big problems, 114–16; as a spiritual movement, 62; spiritual preparations for (*see* spiritual warfare); and working from strengths and interests, 166–68. *See also* hospitality, radically ordinary, barriers to; hospitality, radically ordinary, practices of; table fellowship
hospitality, radically ordinary, barriers to: bad habits and hidden sin, 214–15; counterfeit hospitality, 70, 71, 215–16; a false sense of entitlement based on gifts and interests, 214; the idols of achievement and acquisition, 216–18
hospitality, radically ordinary, practices of: don't accuse of ill will people who hold to a different theology, 56–58; know why it matters most that we are made in God's image, 58–62; pray that

Scripture Index